# The Black Panties:

## Tales of Animal Mischief
### and
### Veterinary Intrigue

T0151085

## Monica Mansfield, D.V.M.

Beanpole Books
**2006**

*The name of the town where the stories occurred has been changed. Owners and most pet names have been changed.*

Beanpole Books
P.O. Box 242
Midway, Florida 32343

Printed in the United States of America on acid-free paper
First Edition

Editor: Anna Chinappi
Cover and interior art work: Sue Ellen Wilson
Cover design: Linda Callahan

ISBN10: 0-9667359-3-5
ISBN 13: 978-0-9667359-3-2

*In loving memory of Susana Napier, Malcolm Mansfield,*
*Lynn Mills, Becky McKee, Maryanne Kern, Maureen Henrickson,*
*Mike Waye and Dan Stryer, the recent losses of whom have left a huge hole.*
*Each individual an extraordinary person.*

## Acknowledgments

First and foremost I thank my incredible husband Keith and our precious sons Phil and Greg. This couldn't have come together without your love, support, excellent ideas and takeout dinners. Thanks to my publisher Linda Hill for her generous heart, for believing in me and for taking me on board. Thanks to Sue Ellen Wilson for her moving illustrations and for our friendship that we've shared since grade school. Thanks to editor Anna Chinappi for her wise and encouraging comments. Thank you to Nick Schatzle, one of the finest human beings I've met and the best mentor one could hope for. Thanks also to Marybeth Camp and Becky Person, who together became Beth in these stories. Thanks to Melanie Eresian, whose positive energy, terrific ideas and typing skills helped get this book started early on. Thanks to my author friend Laurie Foos and to the individuals in her writers group at Borders who watered, fed, pruned and gave vitamins to my work. Thanks to author and friend Laurel King, who helped immensely with my making it to the finish line in better form. Thanks to the many devoted pet owners and animal empathicos over the years and the animals they have entrusted to my care, especially those in these stories. Thanks to my teachers and classmates at Cornell's New York State College of Veterinary Medicine.

Thanks to Ron and Barbara Mosher for their generosity and support. Thank you to John Cooley of the Loon Preservation Committee in Moultonboro, NH, for confirming the accuracy of my loon observations. Thanks to the many veterinarians and coworkers through the years I have worked with and learned from. Thanks to Mike Robinson's warm and wonderful staff at Medway Animal Hospital, whose love, validation and all-around good karma are great gifts. Alice Mansfield has been a reader of these stories, a consultant and an absolutely perfect mother-in-law. Thanks to Harriet Stanley and to Cheryl Hoenemeyer, each willing rehabilitators to various needy animals over the years. Thank you to the voices that urged me early on to write: Bill Beller, Nancy Lamond and my tenth-grade teacher, Carolyn Kassabian. Thanks to my other test readers: Maria Sheehan, Nora Bouchard and Shelly Waxman. Thanks to the SMC staff—Liz Poplawski, Marc Serra, Lori Bergman, Bill Nay and Maria Sheehan—for consulting on some of this book's finer points and for all your support. Thanks to my amazing siblings Kathleen Bors, Judy Davis and Phil Bors and to the friends in my life I consider like family. Thanks to Doug and Ian Mansfield. Thanks to my earth angels whose lives reflect a special breed of selfless love: Susana Napier, Anne Cullen, Alice Mansfield, Nora Bouchard and Andrea Looney. Thanks to my dear friend Lennie Peterson, who helped on so many levels. Thanks to the wonderfully supportive Mike and Stacey Gianfriddo. Thank you to the many musicians who greatly inspire me and feed my creative writing soul, especially Willy Porter, Ellis Paul, Chris Trapper, Merrie Amsterburg, Clutch Grabwell and Turtlebone.

# PROLOGUE

Situated in the foothills of New Hampshire's White Mountains, the region's scenery was spectacular at almost every turn. Ceaseless rows of conifers and elms, oaks and maples lined the mountain highway leading to Norwich as stalwart as palace soldiers yet as welcoming as Southern belles. Tantalizing glimpses of the great mountain peaks ahead were the carrot before the horse's nose as my car climbed northward on my passage into town. The first few times I drove there for my job interview and thereafter, the awe seeped in like music, like love, a visceral emotion linked to that perfect view from the highway.

From the Norwich exit, the ride quickly became a rural and quiet roadway. A right hand turn after the Java Hut, the Home of the Homemade Donut, and there was the historic Jones Covered Bridge. Passage through this sturdy road piece was the most direct way onto Smith Farm Road in Norwich, the beautiful street that led to the center of this small town. Its greeting sign, "One Lane Bridge," excited me for it would soon be my turn to hear the hum of the wooden slats under the car wheels. Often, as I drove through this wooden structure, I imagined myself in a distant past, yielding to an oncoming horse and buggy. Many of New England's wooden bridges were built in the early 1800s, this one in 1850. In the old days, I was told, throughout New England these were called kissing bridges, as teens walking home from Sunday church services were safe from prying eyes for the short term.

The Norwich Animal Hospital where I worked was three miles down Smith Farm Road next to the town common. Driving down this road in the fall of 1987, the start of that formative year of my veterinary career, I imagined the modern family stories connected to the old classic New England capes and pretty Victorians with their wraparound porches, large patio swings and the occasional cat resting on the rail. Often, when on call, I drove home in a hurry in order to be near my phone and seeing these porches incited envy as I fancied the relaxed lives of the residents in these houses, with my made-up scenarios about them, they with their predictable hours at their straight-forward jobs. I was jealous that they could potentially just sit and enjoy a cup of coffee on their porches, reading the newspaper, no hurry or flurry. It's not that I frequently saw anyone doing so but my fantasy remained.

# ONE

## *BUGSY*

For Nick and me, it was a competition first thing each morning. By seven a.m., the first to arrive laid claim to the title of Mop Master and our early cleaning routine began with our leaving the waiting room floor sparkly and mud-free and the hospital clean and fresh. Nick had never hired a kennel worker nor required his receptionist to do the primary hospital disinfecting or cage cleaning, so those tasks were ones he and I shared.

"Call me frugal," he would say, "but I feel like I provide better care if I see what the animals have eaten and produced. Making this place shine gives me great pride."

That was often a quiet hour before the rush of the day. We tended to our hospitalized patients, usually three or four per night, told corny jokes and maintained the orderly and sanitary conditions of the kennel in Nick's charming country veterinary clinic, one he had designed and helped build from the ground up. His idea had been to move away from the city in the latter decade of his veterinary career to the magnificent countryside of the New Hampshire White Mountain chain, off the beaten path, seeing patients a couple of days a week, enough to keep his hand in it. However, his practice had rapidly grown in the ten years he had owned it, overwhelming him. Seven nights a week on call, juggling the medical cases, never feeling relaxed if he went away for an overnight. He needed an extra set of veterinary hands and that's where I had come in.

I had endured a harrowing three months with a different employer on my first job out of veterinary school, a fledgling flying out of the nest with my new wings clipped. Nick saved the part of my life that was a veterinarian. And with that, I salvaged my self-respect. The veterinarian for whom I first worked used intimidation and criticism and provided no support as I flailed. When any problems arose, the silent treatment, rolled eyeballs and slammed cabinet doors were the only resultant teachable moments. "You don't know how to think like a veterinarian," was told to me my second week on the job. I found out after I quit that several other young veterinarians before me had passed through with similarly bruised psyches but this offered me little consolation. After all the hard work and years of schooling to pursue a childhood dream to make sick animals well—and I was left disillusioned and pained. I soul-searched to learn if I was truly cut out for the profession or whether I had just started off with the wrong person. It was hard to see past my dejection into the possibilities before me.

Nick, the antithesis of my first boss, welcomed me with open arms, celebrating my strengths as a complement to his. Thank God I had found him. I was the only applicant for the job—I saw the small index card on a bulletin board at a continuing education meeting I attended after I quit that first job. It said: "Seeking full-time small animal veterinarian in White Mountain region of New Hampshire. Small staff and homey atmosphere." We hit it right off but I had to think about it for a while since the job would pull me a hundred miles away from my longtime boyfriend Keith. I eventually realized that I desperately needed a nurturing job experience next.

When I started with Nick, he saw my rapport with the clients as a boon and welcomed my enthusiasm for challenging medical cases, cases he did not particularly enjoy himself. Understanding my prior situation and rather than leaving me stranded, he gently guided me through the finer points of his surgical and anesthetic techniques—good, safe ones. He taught me how to insert an endotracheal breathing tube with no assistance, a technique that served me well in the wee hours of the night alone, removing porcupine quills from dogs or suturing lacerations. Nick spoke warmly and enthusiastically about me to his clients, often within my earshot, and his praise went a long way toward healing my wounds, helping me believe I was good enough.

"Good morning, good morning!" There was a lift in Nick's step as he mopped the lobby floor when I walked in to work one unseasonably balmy Monday morning a month after I began working there. He and his wife Gail would be leaving that night for a ten-day vacation in Rhode Island. There was to be a boat show where Nick could run his hand along the hull of an Egg Harbor powerboat or ogle at the Island Packet forty-foot sailboat of his dreams. He would imagine himself someday in retirement, behind the helm, living off the coast of Maine, no phones, just a well-deserved rest. He and Gail made plans to stroll along a famous walkway in Newport with breathtaking views of the mansions on the cliffs high above the water. I knew he couldn't wait to go.

"So how was the weekend for you, Nick? Many calls?" I put my bag down on the bench in the waiting room and unbuttoned my jacket. The room smelled good, lemon-scented and clean.

"Not a lot. I had an interesting pinning to do Saturday. Little shih tzu jumped from the front window of his owners' pickup truck. Nice complicated femoral fracture. I got it done right away that afternoon." Nick always seemed so unassuming, with no worries when it came to things like this.

"Wish I'd been in town this weekend to see it." I felt that stab of insecurity again as I realized this surgery would have been beyond my abilities. I wished there was a way to have acquired more hands-on orthopedic surgery in school. It would have been difficult for our professors to perfect that skill among all the others we were supposed to be learning. Perhaps our vet school exposure was meant for us to see who had the "bug," the drive, the aptitude to pursue that as a specialty with specific training. I wished it came easy for me but instead surgery was scary. The way a body system looked in a textbook and the way it is when you are peering into an opened cavity lit by powerful surgery lamps were two completely different things. Concealed blood vessels, excessive body fat confounding proper suture technique, adhesions from prior procedures to change the landscape of the insides and strange anatomical variants all created tension in my little surgeon's core. There is no wiggle room or fudge factor in surgery. You can't "kind-of" do it properly, can't zone out. Absolute attention to detail and anatomy at all times is vital. Even the act of fishing around for the uterine horns during a routine spay could turn into a challenge until one was a seasoned surgeon. And then there was the issue of monitoring anesthesia simultaneously. Certainly not a relaxed time. Thank goodness there are sets of veterinarians who love performing surgery, live for the thrill, for putting things back together again, the high level of skill required to be a specialist. For me, I definitely leaned more naturally to being a medicine person than a surgery person, finding my excitement in putting the medical clues and lab work puzzle together into a diagnosis. Here in such a rural area, some animals still needed fracture repairs and we general practitioners needed a plan. I absorbed as much as possible from Nick's experience. Still, I fervently wished to be naturally skilled and confident in all aspects of veterinary medicine, capable of dealing with most anything that came my way in this remote region.

"I'll look the dog over, Nick, and feed him for you," I called as I walked through the treatment room back to the kennel. I couldn't wait to see our patient and see Nick's handiwork, at least on the X-rays. The kennel room's concrete walls and cement floor were painted the same calming pale blue and the room bore the signature aroma of bleach. Connected through the kennel room's back door were four outdoor runs, each individually fenced, with a secondary fence surrounding the entire set of runs. These too were meticulously cleaned and maintained by Nick. The steam from the hot water used to hose down the runs would rise to his khaki-panted knees. Every morning, undaunted even by winter's chill, Nick faithfully completed these chores in a short-sleeved, V-neck white T-shirt that would later be topped by a light-blue, side-snapped lab coat when the day's appointments began.

My eyes settled on the only patient in the clinic. The cage card read

Bugsy Lafleur. Staring back at me was an eight-pound wad of tangled white and brown fur. The hair parted slightly to reveal two brown eyes and a dark dot of a nose. An obvious underbite in which the lower teeth jutted precipitously forward, completely covering the upper lip, feigned the appearance of a ferocious dog, yet Bugsy's looks belied his sweet demeanor. Bugsy welcomed my attentions with a slow sweep of his tail and a reach for my face with his wide tongue. He sweetly whined at me with endearing little grunts, begging for my attentions. His right leg dragged behind him, still bandaged in a splint covered in blue Vet-wrap.

"Oh, Bugsy," I cajoled, "what happened to you? You're just a sweet little muffin, aren't you?" I gently picked him up and supporting the leg, moved him to the treatment table where I had already placed a big towel, giving him better traction. My exam revealed that all his vital signs that morning were normal and he kept his eyes fixed on my face. If I leaned too close to his, that tongue would sneak out and try to connect. Bugsy was indeed hungry for breakfast when I put him back in his cage. I laughed as I watched him savor each remaining morsel from the packet of moist chunks his owners apparently had left for him, his mouth enthusiastically searching the stainless bowl for straggler bites. He flipped his tongue methodically around his lip edges, hoping for a retained speck.

"Nick," I walked to the next room, "that is one of the ugliest dogs I have ever seen!"

"Isn't he, though?" he laughed. "The owners really love that dog, but they joke about his appearance too. He's a good dog, very cooperative."

"He's awesome, quite a character, I can see. And we can't bathe him before he goes home because of the bandage, can we?"

"Yeaaaah, I guess. I just hate to send dogs home dirty. It's like a business card. Every time an animal goes home clean, people remember that." Nick's policy of washing every hospitalized patient the morning it went home was another task he took upon himself. Every sickie, every spay, every neuter—all were washed. He kept most animals overnight the day of surgery. That way he was sure the recovery went well and since his house was attached to the clinic, he would do another walk-through check of all the patients before he went to sleep at night.

"Let me show you the X-rays," Nick said, pulling the films off the viewer. "I'm pretty proud of this. I had to put the pin in this way so that it would stay in place. You can see on the follow-up films that it looks well-seated. The bones were in a couple pieces, kind of like a jigsaw puzzle."

"Nice job, Nick! What a mess! I'm glad it was you, not me, putting that back together." I was relieved that all was well, especially since Nick was about to take off. I wouldn't have been able to do this. How did he have enough hands to pull it together and know what went where and watch the anesthesia all at the same time? He laughed off my incredulity.

Nick sent Bugsy home that day with strict instructions to keep his activity to a minimum, keeping him in a crate or an upside down playpen. Bugsy simultaneously embellished wet, wide kisses on his delighted owners Jamie and Ed and wiggled his happy rear end when they came to take him home.

Nick and Gail left that evening for their vacation and I dug my heels in for what I hoped to be a fairly uneventful ride, me the captain of the ship for my first long stretch alone since I'd joined the practice. Even when Nick wasn't the one taking calls, if I was really, really stuck and he was there, I always knew I could call him when it was my night or weekend. My floatation device was leaving town and I'd have to prove how well my swim lessons would hold me up.

The days went quickly that first week and save for one minor hit-by-car accident, the emergency calls were light, all things that I could handle. By Friday morning, the ominous feeling was lifting. I found myself humming the way Nick always did as I ran the early morning mop, Mop Master for the entire week, proud of myself for keeping up with all my responsibilities and still holding it all together. When the phone rang, I knew that sacred first hour of the day was over.

Before long, our receptionist Beth was on duty and took over the phone calls. Within moments, in the sweetest of voices and with the brightest of smiles, she informed me that Jamie Lafleur was on the phone. "She was wondering if we could squeeze her in since Bugsy's pin is sticking out through the top of the bandage."

My high spirits deflated. Not an orthopedic problem for me! Oh God. What should I do? Maybe they were wrong. Sometimes owners misinterpret things. Maybe the bandage was just bunched up. How many times have we seen what the owner thought was a tick and it was really a little skin tag they were trying to pull off?

"Have them come in as soon as they can, Beth, and plan on leaving him here, just in case. Hopefully he hasn't eaten." I managed to sound in-charge, although I had no idea what I was going to do if the situation was as I imagined. With all my heart I hoped the owner was mistaken.

Jamie arrived with Bugsy within minutes before any of my scheduled appointments. Good-humored, she remained undisturbed. In fact, she brought with her a wave of good cheer.

"Good morning, Jamie," I greeted her first, maintaining a calm veneer despite the growing knot in my stomach. "What's going on?"

And there it was. The pin. Taunting me. Indeed sticking out through the top of the now-dirty bandage material by about two inches, fully exposed to the environment.

"I just noticed it this morning when we got up, Dr. Bors," Jamie explained helpfully.

"Wow. How quiet has he been? Has he been crated?" I was stalling, begging my mind to tell me what to do. What now? I fiddled with the earpieces of my stethoscope as if they could make a magic genie appear to fix this mess if I rubbed them enough.

"Well, we're probably guilty there. We didn't get a crate the way Dr. Schatzle had told us to because we felt bad for him, so Bugsy has probably been moving around more than he should. Ed caught him jumping off the couch last night. Do you think that could have something to do with it?" She turned her cheek toward her shoulder and winced a little.

Yeah, it coulda, the stressed-out alter ego inside my head dared me to say aloud, What do *you* think? "Could have, Jamie," I spoke sweetly, "Dr. Schatzle showed me the X-rays and how nicely everything came together for him, so it was pretty well-seated after surgery. He was actually quite pleased with the surgery. He did a great job."

"I'm not surprised. We don't have kids and Bugsy is like a spoiled child to us. My husband felt it most unkind to confine him the way Dr. Schatzle had told us to. I guess we learned a hard lesson. It's just that he's always on Ed's or my lap all the time, and we thought he'd be miserable. That's why he broke it in the first place—he was on Ed's lap behind the steering wheel in the pickup truck and jumped down when the door opened." Jamie was smiling in her personable way, but she turned her head downward as she expressed her regret. I glanced briefly at their large-wheeled, Ford F250 with passenger cab in the parking lot and noticed the distance those little legs had tumbled in the original fall. Pickup trucks were a common mode of transportation in Norwich, compatible with snowplows for the upcoming winter season I was forewarned about.

"Well, Jamie, I'll take him in and snap another set of X-rays. The problem is that I can't simply push the pin back in, since it's contaminated. I think the fracture is way too weak after only six days. And I'd probably need some help with the surgery myself." My head was spinning. What to do? There was no way in the world I could handle this surgery on my own, even if I had Nick's level of experience. How had Nick ever repaired this break on his own in the first place? Even with another set of hands scrubbed in, I wouldn't know how to piece this together well enough to help Bugsy. And then I'd need someone to mind the anesthesia. Plus I had appointments scheduled all day, alone and no extra staff, so we would need to reshuffle schedules all around. My stomach tightened. When I next opened my mouth, I would need a plan, something intelligent to say to Jamie. In the back of my mind, I remembered Nick having once mentioned a veterinarian to the south with considerable orthopedic experience to whom he sometimes referred knee injury repairs. I recalled Nick's telling me of this doctor's vast collection of used human hospital equipment he bought at auction, his endoscopes and monitoring machines. Thank goodness Nick and I had that conversation and that my anxiety fog had cleared enough to bring it back. Maybe this was my lifeboat.

"What I'll do is make a phone call to a hospital I believe is in Triton," I told Jamie, a new lease sparked in my veterinary soul. "One of the doctors there does really well with tough surgical problems. Dr. Schatzle told me about him." I grasped again at Nick's conversation in my head, and the name came to me, Dr. Abbey. Yes, that was it. My renewed hopes were simply that Dr. Abbey could fit Bugsy into his schedule. If he wasn't there, I would have to send the owners on a three-hour trip to Tufts Veterinary School outside of Boston.

"I understand. I was afraid of this." Her lack of makeup and simple windblown hairstyle reflected a woman at ease with herself and family—

a comfortable, pleasant person I guessed. Or someone who had simply rushed out the door to get to the vet's office. I liked her warmth and enthusiasm. And her honesty made our job much easier. How could you fault someone for loving their animal too much?

"Has he eaten this morning?" I patted his head and rubbed behind Bugsy's flopped-over ear.

"Luckily, no, I was just preparing his breakfast when I noticed."

"Great, I'll call you later when I know more, Jamie." I was trying to create a plan for the day in my mind as I carried Bugsy, gingerly supporting his injured leg. His tongue went into action, as though operated by a super-charged battery. "Good boy, Bugsy, good boy."

I needed to quickly take new X-rays before my morning appointments arrived. I would have to be able to describe the pin's location and status to Dr. Abbey on the phone. When I developed the films, I groaned. The surgery would be even tougher the second time. To my pleasant surprise, Beth had the all-important phone number waiting for me up front. In fact, she said she could have told me all along Dr. Abbey was the expert I was looking for. He was well known in the area, too, for his good work. Why, she assumed from the second she took the phone call that I would be referring our little friend to him and was so sorry I didn't know. She had presumed I felt the same way, so she felt no angst over the whole situation, she said. Beth was certain Nick would have sent this case too had it been him dealing with it. Validated, humbled and a little nervous, I called to introduce myself to Dr. Abbey in Triton, and he was there, thank goodness. I explained our sad tale and detailed the pin's wanderlust.

"I'd be happy to help you out, Monica," he said in a jovial voice as if he'd known me for years. Such sweet music to my ears. "How about if we do the surgery together here at my practice. Can you be here at one?"

"Sure, I can't thank you enough!" I grinned widely and silently danced a move that rivaled the best of the NFL touchdown spike displays.

"Oh, wait'll they see my bill," he laughed. This must have been an ongoing joke, as Nick had once told me the area vets were quite willing to lend a hand to one another when asked, often at a nominal cost, if any.

Sweet relief flooded my veins and this morning's trepidation became action. I would wear my proverbial roller skates for the morning appointments, extra motivated to keep things on track. I was starting off behind, but Beth could rearrange some of my appointments. Most people didn't mind changing when an emergency arose. Were it their own animal, they would want the same done for them. Fortunately, we weren't overbooked, and most cases were fairly routine that day.

I informed Jamie of our plan, and, at lunchtime I put a tranquil Bugsy into a travel cage and headed south, an agent on an important mission. The hospital was easy to find, and I was there in less than half an hour. With stars in my eyes, I walked into Dr. Abbey's surgical suite—a large, modern space with machinery here and monitors there. Long tubes and an endoscope hung from a special hook on the wall and each of the two surgery tables were bedecked with equipment to amplify all the respirations and heart patterns as best as was available. Large white cabinet doors were labeled and ordered. Official-looking glass windows separated the surgery suite from the next room, allowing observers. Dr. Abbey welcomed me like I was a long lost niece. We straightaway anesthetized Bugsy. I watched Dr. Abbey perform magic that day, my Knight in Shining Armor, as he made an involved surgery appear effortless, all in good cheer. Bone fragments were gently coaxed into place, then secured with two new, sterile pins that crisscrossed, making their chances of slippage minimal, no matter how much Bugsy ignored the doctor's instructions. A couple of thin wires skillfully placed around the pinned bone and the masterpiece was ready to be sewn back together. Pink Floyd's "Dark Side of the Moon" wafted through the stereo speakers, a muse for this surgeon's hands, he told me. In fact, any complicated surgery always got treated to this tape, as all good outcomes occurred during its playing, he laughed. I loved the idea that this man of steel pins was also inspired and recharged by the universal language the way I was. I would remember that as I settled into my own surgery routines, allowing myself tunes that improved my sense of well being. I supposed many of us had our comfort zones and lucky items we relied on, perhaps similar to a baseball player's ritualistic routine. For me, it was the maroon dangly earrings that I usually wore on the days I knew I was the scheduled surgeon. What a thrill it was here, scrubbed in, a second set of hands and made to feel a valuable part of this advanced surgery. I am certain, however, that Dr. Abbey would have managed just fine without me. He invited me to close the final layer of skin. I thanked him profusely for all he had done, gushing about how he had really come through for us and how could I ever return the favor. Within two hours from the time I arrived at Triton, Bugsy was recovering from the anesthetic and the sleepy dog and I drove the twenty-six-minute ride back to Norwich in time for my remaining afternoon appointments. Not even the foreboding chill in the air and the naked tree branches fazed me now. It was all good. My relief and gratitude for Dr. Abbey's help filled me as I raced through the paces of the afternoon appointments, mission accomplished. I had had a revelation that day, something that Nick had been telling me all along, that it was perfectly all right to share the benefit of someone else's skill and talents, taking the pressure off myself to be perfect at everything at all times. Bugsy rested in a cozy cage, blanket under him, drugs on board to keep him comfortable and dozy.

The next day, at the time of Bugsy's discharge, I asked Jamie, "Now, what arrangement will you have for his confinement when you get home?" I cradled Bugsy, knowing I'd have to give him back soon. I patted his forehead and smoothed the hair from his eyes.

"We'll do the upside down playpen or we can keep him in the bathroom. I swear, no couches this time!" Impassioned, she traced an x on her chest, crossing her heart.

Beaming as usual, she finished, "Thanks for taking such good care of our baby!"

He was a baby, preferring the comfort of his caregivers' arms over the cage any day. He snuggled his head into the crook of my elbow while twisting his chin skyward, exuding little whimpers, tempting me to cuddle him indefinitely. It hadn't taken long to fall under Bugsy's spell and Beth and I were each showered by his generous tongue before he left.


Nick returned from his trip right on schedule, refreshed and relaxed. His eyes sparkled as he described the wide variety of boats he had drooled over at the show. "One of these days when I retire, I'll have one of those boats," he fancied. He had shared his dream with me before, so I knew how this vacation fed his soul.

"Before you came, Dr. B, I could never have taken a trip for so long. I'm so glad you joined the practice," he bubbled.

While it had been a busy time for me as the solo doctor, there had been no new crises after Bugsy. Nick was surprised when I told him about the pin slippage but pleased with the results of the second surgery. He would call Dr. Abbey that day to also thank him. We hatched a plan to have some gourmet cookies delivered to Dr. Abbey's practice.

Bugsy's recheck appointment date came. "The leg looks great, Jamie," I told her. Bugsy wiggled and whined for my attention. "How's he been doing?" I took him in my arms and told him how happy I was to see him.

Jamie swatted at a wisp of her brown hair that had fallen across one eye. "Good. We're keeping him confined in the bathroom when we're not home and the playpen other times. He cries when he sees us from his jail cell." She reported. "You know, though, this morning he didn't want to eat breakfast, and he did vomit once."

"Hmmm." I inserted a thermometer into his behind. "I wonder if he could have picked up a virus. Has he been around other dogs? Change of diet?"

"Nothing, other than being in the hospital."

"Well, let's see how it goes. Maybe his antibiotic is making his stomach queasy. Let's put him on a bland diet for the next few days, boiled hamburger and rice, in small amounts. See how he holds it down and let us know if he's not steadily more comfortable in a day or two." This sounded like a good plan—his spirits were good, and his abdomen palpated normally.

Instead of his symptoms improving, Bugsy refused to eat the next day and became uncharacteristically depressed. This guy was not well. When Jamie brought him back that day, there were no loving, licking attempts, just a head that hung heavy on the exam table. Jamie understood the need to re-hospitalize our little friend.

I snapped some radiographs and showed them to Nick, who was as concerned as I felt. "Look at his stomach, Nick. It's really thickened and irritated."

"Yup, yup, and it looks full even though he hasn't eaten in two days. There's got to be something in there that will have to come out. This part sure doesn't look like food, but it isn't stomach mucosa either."

While I saw appointments, Nick gave Bugsy some barium dye.

"Look at these, Dr. B!" He displayed some films for me to see as I entered the treatment room. "I only had to do two sets of X-rays. Of course, our little dog here decided to share some of his barium with me." Nick's cheek and chin were smeared white where Bugsy, even feeling sick as he was, had licked him.

"How'd you get those done so fast?" I asked, unaware and hoping he hadn't needed a hand.

"Oh, no trouble, no trouble. I only needed to take two views, fifteen minutes apart to see this. No all day affair this time." During a barium swallow, it was often necessary to snap a series of films to outline any suspect areas, which could take all day.

Nick's films showed a large, obvious spaghetti-like jumbled mass in the stomach. I wondered what that could be, most likely a foreign object the dog had eaten. As well, as a completely separate issue, Bugsy's esophagus, the muscle that carried food down the throat, was pinched at its lower portion where it entered the stomach. In response to the abnormal narrowing, the esophagus ballooned ahead of it.

"I saw this once in a vet school lecture!" I was really glad for Dr. Flanders's touching on this once in class and glad I was paying attention to the lecture that day. It had sounded so esoteric at the time; he had even told us this was pretty rare. "Nick, I think Bugsy could have an esophageal stricture and a secondarily widened esophagus at that location. Do you think that could be a result of any of the anesthesias for his surgeries?"

"That's odd . . . I don't know. That would be hard to believe. Why, I don't think I've ever seen an esophageal stricture, at least that I've known about." He smiled. "Gee, I'm not sure I would have caught that. I don't know its significance in this case . . . glad I can use your brain to help unravel this little mystery." His quiet words and faith were a soothing salve.

"I guess he needs an exploratory, huh? There's no question there's something in there." I winced. Poor Bugs. Another procedure. Another surgery.

"It goes on and on with this dog," he agreed. I relaxed, knowing that if we did this today, Nick would deftly explore Bugsy's intestines in surgery while I kept up with appointments. I hadn't at that point even performed a stomach exploratory on a real patient—we had had some experience in vet school on our surgery rotation—and I wasn't thinking I wanted Bugs to be my first. Nick could be quicker about doing the procedure than I ever could and he preferred surgery anyhow to seeing appointments. We weren't quite sure what to do about the esophagus but we knew the foreign body was a priority and it quickly needed to be dealt with. We would take care of this and hope time would heal the esophagus.

On the phone, Jamie consented to the surgery. What other choice did we have? Her voice wasn't laughing this time. She asked me to give Bugsy a kiss. When I went to the back room to do just that, Nick already had his head leaned inside Bugsy's cage, pre-empting my efforts. I walked back out up front, feeling fortunate to have him as my example.

The anticipation of what Nick would discover was tempered by my need to keep on track with appointments. Nick began the exploratory that afternoon and before long, he called for Beth to hurry up and come get me. I ran back, hoping there wasn't an anesthetic crisis.

"Monica, look what was in the stomach! I need you to help me remove the dirty part." Nick used a hemostat to pull the contaminated stomach contents and I tried to keep them from touching or dripping on the surgical site. Shortly, we had delivered into the world a large wad of thick, braided, bile-stained strings.

Nick couldn't wait for me to ask Jamie about this most unusual finding. He was happy for me to do the telephone part and I was happy for him to do the surgery part.

"Bugsy's doing well so far," I called her while Nick sewed up our patient. "You're not gonna believe what was in his stomach—these look like mop strings or something like that. We'll save them for you to see."

"Mop strings?!? You're kidding! What did he . . .? How could he . . .? Oh my God! I had the mop in the bathroom one day last week. He must have chewed it. That was right before the vomiting started. Oh my God! I was using bleach to do the floors too. Oh my God!" It saddened me to hear the distress in her voice.

Like turning on a light, an answer came to me. The stricture of the esophagus—it was probably a chemical burn from the bleach as the strings were swallowed. I would confirm that later with a phone call to poison control. I hated to bring this up with Jamie no matter how gently it was said.

"Well, Jamie, those mop strings wouldn't have passed through the intestines on their own, so their removal is at least half the battle." I told her about the other problem on the X-rays, that narrowing of the esophagus where it entered the stomach. "Strictures are quite uncommon, but some heal quickly and are well-managed with small, soft meals like ground baby food. Some of these strictures, however, need another anesthetic procedure to widen the esophagus—it's called a bougienage."

"I feel like such a terrible owner! It's all been our fault, we baby him too much, but we just love that little guy!"

"Try not to be so hard on yourself, Jamie. Dogs are unpredictable. Looking at his jaws, who'd have ever thought this guy could be capable of devouring those strings? I don't know how he did it." I wished I could give Jamie a hug over the phone and let her know that she was an extremely caring owner who had been faced with a series of unlucky events. Personally, I felt so much better that we had been able to actually correct the cause of the vomiting before that problem became life threatening.

We initially took a conservative approach with the esophageal stricture, allowing Bugsy's stomach some time to heal from the mop-string extraction. By eating only pureed food with his front legs elevated on a stepladder, food could pass by the constricted region easily and Bugsy was eating and holding down his food. After one week, we attempted a more solid, canned food. However, the chunkier food was regurgitated, so it was back to the drawing board.

Nick wondered how I knew so much about the procedure to surgically correct the tightening of the esophagus. A special type of tube, the bougienage, passed under anesthesia, is progressively widened or ballooned to slowly stretch the narrowed portion. I remembered this from the class lecture, primarily because my irreverent lab partner, Tim, clung to the curious sound of the French word "bougienage" and found a way to weave it nonsensically into nearly every conversation we had over the next few days ("I had too much bougienage last night" or "I laughed so hard, my bougienage hurts" and "quit hogging all the bougienage"), maybe to make himself sound erudite, perhaps to tease me, but mostly to earn a goofy smile from me. In terms of performing this on Bugsy, I now knew right away who to call.

Dr. Abbey was cordial and comforting. "Oh, I have all sorts of toys here, including a bougienage. Never had the chance to use it before! Sort of a hobby with me to collect this stuff. Who knows when I'll ever have occasion to play with it again?" he laughed. "Besides, you're keeping my life very interesting up there! Same dog, huh? Well, send them my way, but only if you send some more of those delicious cookies along. And let me know if there's anything else I can do for you. I enjoy it. Monica, you've been a lot of fun to work with." Fun? I blushed while I laughed, appreciating his compliment, but my worry over this case these past weeks did not feel so light and airy. Instead, I wore like a scarf that sometimes overwhelming burden of responsibility that I hadn't counted on before I walked through the door of my first job as a vet.

Nothing about Bugsy's case had been routine. In my head I silently thanked Dr. Flanders at Cornell again for his teaching. Jamie brought Bugsy to Dr. Abbey for his bougienage procedure. She reported that the doctor was quite optimistic for a favorable outcome and that the narrowing seemed to have been easily corrected during the procedure. Finally, after two weeks, Bugsy was well again. He was eating and acting normally and the leg bandage and various sutures were easily removed.

One month later, it was time to radiograph the leg again for evidence of bone healing. Were the fracture healed well enough on the films, general anesthesia was to be given to Bugsy again for the fifth time and Nick was to remove the pins that Dr. Abbey had placed. In some fractures, like Bugsy's, it was best to remove the pin hardware once healing was complete and the repair site stable with a good bone callous formed.

"We've been really conscientious with everything. Murphy's Law has been overtested and proven to be alive and well on Bugsy," Jamie assured me as she dropped him off, her relaxed expression back again. "But he's able to use that leg as if nothing happened. You should see him in the yard, Monica. He dances, I swear, he's so happy."

"You've fasted him, right?" I checked with her as a formality, glancing up since I knew that she knew the routine.

"Yes, yes. I'm a pro now. He's had no food or water after dinnertime last night so he doesn't choke under anesthesia," she recited in a voice that sounded just like Beth.

"Great. Don't worry," I laughed, "we'll call you when we're all done." I held Bugsy and waved his front paw at his departing mom. I promised him this would be the last episode he'd have to go through. He licked the air, attempting to connect with my cheek, then burrowed his head in my elbow crook.

The radiographs of the fracture site looked super, with evidence of strong bone healing and stability at the fracture site. I helped Nick administer the anesthetic and watched him quickly locate and remove the pin ends using sterile procedure and slide them out.

Bugsy wakened steadily and was ready for his breathing tube to come out. Moments after I removed the tube, however, Bugsy began dry heaving. I quickly positioned him at a declining angle with his head pointing downward so that any vomit would not be choked back into his lungs.

"Poor guy. Jamie was sure he was fasted this morning, Nick." I steadied and stroked the delirious body, leaning close to him, talking softly in his ear. Hopefully he would recognize my voice and it would soothe him.

Then, like Mt. Fuji erupting, voluminous amounts of a brown, fetid mess spewed out of Bugsy's mouth inches from my nose. Its tubular appearance and fetid smell perfectly resembled a dog's bowel movement.

"Oh, gross! That looks like poop!" I called as I stood up straight.

Nick sniffed the bucket it had landed in. "It *is* poop."

"Uhhh . . ." I gagged involuntarily and, re-tasting my lunch, headed to the big trashcan across the room, hovering, taking Bugsy in my arms, still supporting him at an angle. I envisioned the dog and I vomiting in unison as my stomach was ready to empty its contents too. It was certainly not that the sight or smell of dog feces bothered me—I dealt with that in all its various contortions on a daily basis. It was the surprise mode of delivery whizzing past my face, nearly in my face, that threw my senses off guard.

"Fun's fun! Now don't make me clean up two messes, Monica," Nick teased. "You do want to keep holding him downward like that, though, until he's fully awake. Wouldn't want him to inhale this stuff." I recovered quickly but, of course, that wasn't the last I heard of it with Nick's ribbing me.

Jamie, once again, had trouble believing me at first when I told her about Bugsy's episode. We surmised he had been so hungry that he had recycled his morning prize out in the yard. I assured Jamie that, other than that being so disgusting, all was well, and we should be all set from this point.

Unfortunately I was wrong. Within three days, Bugsy developed a soft, gurgly cough. He still felt like eating and his leg was doing great but he rattled out a quiet cough every few moments.

"All right, we're back again," Jamie said, resigned. Her eyes showed their lines of concern. "We will soon own a room in this hospital with a plaque over the door," she tried to joke. "Why is he coughing?"

I knew before I placed the stethoscope on his chest what must have happened.

I felt so bad for them for all their difficulties, and now there was more. How could such an innocent little dog get himself into so much trouble? Were he human, he would probably be the quiet, impish child who stuck pudding into the tape flap of a VCR machine, then walked away as if nothing had happened.

I listened to his lungs and tried to keep the heaviness I felt out of my voice. "Parts of his lungs sound moist, and I suspect aspiration pneumonia, meaning he may have taken a small amount of his feces into his lungs as he vomited up his stool. The bacteria have set up an infection there. We'll take an X-ray of his chest." I was not going to let this beat him and I told her that. Pneumonias were very serious business and some cases even required transfer to an advanced center for constant oxygen administration. I knew Jamie trusted us to do our best and that she would be hard pressed to make the long trip to a large facility unless absolutely necessary. She was fighting back tears as I left the exam room with Bugsy in my arms.

He coughed with most any movement he made and as I placed Bugsy in a cozy cage, he sputtered a string of coughs. Radiographs showed lung infiltrates consistent with an early pneumonia. We opted to keep Bugsy hospitalized until we had the upper hand on his symptoms. Please, God, after all he's been through, this lung issue was so random, please, please let this trial-ridden little dog pull through, I prayed in my head.

An aggressive course of intravenous antibiotics was given over the course of those five days while I walked on pins and needles. Only once that week was I able to arrive in the morning earlier than Nick, who was himself sneaking in extra-early. Each time I found him straightaway ministering to Bugsy's needs—a new dish of Bugsy's favorite moist food, plumping and freshening of the blankets, a laughing cheek to satisfy that lunging tongue of Bugs. I even caught Nick one morning singing earnestly to Bugs, "How much is that doggy in the window . . . .?" before Nick knew I was in the building. I never teased him about that later because it was so sweet. Perhaps he'd been serenading the dog every day and I didn't want to discourage that. Thankfully, Bugsy never lost his appetite or good spirits. During the days, we would administer his treatments—the vital antibiotics, careful intravenous fluids doses so as not to overload his fragile lungs and vaporizer treatments. A technique to try to move lung junk up and out of the airways, called coupage, was performed several times daily. The sides of his chest were patted vigorously to encourage the expectoration of mucus and muck. Most important was the quiet we were able to provide our little friend. While at home he would indeed be doted on and intensely loved, but here we were assured of rest and very little movement in his high-rise deluxe condo cage, I promised Jamie.

Thankfully, he responded well and quickly. Of all his trials, this was perhaps his smoothest recovery. He continued to charm the entire staff. The cough quieted, and on the fifth day, his follow-up X-rays looked much better, though not perfect. I sighed deeply, thankful once again. Glad for the right antibiotic mix, the body responding, Bugsy getting yet another chance.

It was time for him to go home. For good, I hoped. That was a joyful reunion for Jamie, Ed and their infamous little guy. Bugsy turned to me, then his owners, then back to me in a motion that seemed to say we're all family. I gave him another cuddle and handed him, his tongue lapping the air, back to Jamie.

"Jamie, I truly believe this is the last time here for Bugsy. Just keep him out of trouble and make sure he finishes out his pills. We'll really miss him, you know. You know how special he is, don't you?" I managed.

"My million dollar baby. I think this exam room is the one I'd like you to place the plaque over that says 'sponsored by Bugsy Lafleur'. How about it?" We all laughed, hers leading the rounds, a final release. "I don't know what to say to thank you, Monica, except . . . can I get him groomed yet?" She gently smoothed the tangled fur on his head. Of all of Bugsy's thrilling adventures in the past two months, one of those was not a visit to the groomer.

"One week after the cough is completely gone but that may take some time. Some of these linger for weeks. And have him wear his sweater outside." She agreed.

His scraggly hair would have completely covered his eyes if not held by a blue barrette on top. The hair around his lips was knotted and taken into his mouth as he ate. He resembled, well, a mop.

And that was the last of Bugsy's bad luck. His leg never so much as limped later, his regurgitation problem was solved, and his cough thankfully disappeared in rapid response to medication. Jamie and Ed bought him a doggie seatbelt attachment for trips in the front seat of the pickup truck.

I received a nice card from Jamie after Bugsy was well. "Enclosed are some pictures from when Bugsy was at his worst (those just break my heart!). As you can see, he made a miraculous recovery. We never did make Bugsy get a full-time job to pay off his vet bills. We really appreciate all you guys did for Bugs." Included were a series of photos—before, during and after. From a pathetic-looking ragamuffin sporting a blue cast to the clean, clipped look of another dog whose lower jaw jutted proudly forward.

A healthy Bugsy.

# TWO

## *NICHOLAS THE CAT*

"Well, Nicholas, what brings you in to the clinic today, you handsome boy?" I spoke directly to the generously proportioned cat lounging on the exam room table.

"Doctor, he's been drooling since I first saw him around seven this morning. I was rather worried about it. Other than that, he seems fine," his owner answered sweetly.

Sheila's tan blouse and stylish jeans accented her slender build. With our proximity to the local state college and her apparent age, I guessed her to be a student there. She was impeccably groomed, save for some orange cat hairs dotting the neckline of her shirt.

Nicholas's chin and chest were soaking wet, as if he forgot to turn off a hidden faucet in his mouth. Bubbles formed at the corners of his lips. He, however, remained undisturbed, blissfully rubbing my hand as I patted him, his audible purr inviting me to be his best friend.

"Okay, Nicholas, let me look inside your mouth and see what's going on," I cooed.

A host of potential causes for Nicholas's problem flooded my mind in the few seconds he greeted me before I peered in. The most common cause of drooling in cats I'd seen was small ulcers or abrasions on the tongue from chewing certain house plants, like philodendron or dieffenbachia or else from a respiratory virus. Occasionally, sickly older cats suffering from kidney disease developed tongue ulcers. I remembered the time a profusely drooling cat I examined had a vertebra of a rodent—presumably a mouse—wedged between two of his upper teeth. That had been an easy situation to reverse with a flick of my thumb.

"Nicholas, you share the hospital owner's name, you know that?"

Sheila flashed a smile. "I told Dr. Schatzle that he's named after him but between you and me"—she shrugged one shoulder to her ear—"I just happen to like the name."

"He sure is a cooperative patient." I was startled when I peered inside his mouth, his purr continuing. "Nicholas! You look like you're part snake!"

"Ugh." Sheila's soft smile faded as her face paled.

Nicholas's tongue was split in half smack-dab down the center, from its tip to mid-center. The bloodless whitish edges told me that this injury was at least twelve hours old. "Any idea what he may have done to himself?" I was puzzled. This was the first time I'd seen such a sight.

"I have no idea! Ewww, that's really disgusting." She looked away. The mid-afternoon sunbeam through the window outlined her features, her unease captured as if a model in a Richard Avedon photo.

"Does he go outside?" I hoped for some clue.

"All the time. There's a barn next door that he loves to investigate. He just wants to be out as much as he can. I wish I could keep him in but he'd go nuts, howling and scratching up the door frame to go out."

My best guess was that he split it on a tin can of some sort. Sheila confirmed that he was a tuna fanatic but that he was an equal opportunity food aficionado. A trash can raid was definitely feasible. Nicholas escalated the volume of his purr to the clearly-audible-across-the-room level.

"Who knows what's in that barn and wherever else he goes when he's out."

She shifted her weight and balanced herself against the exam table. She didn't look too well. I wondered if she was picturing her food-motivated trash-picker in the act of acquiring his injury. The small exam rooms in Nick's hospital, though tidy and welcoming, did not have chairs ("So the owners pay attention," he once told me. "Besides, I hardly ever keep people waiting.") though I wished for a seat in her case. Shelia didn't seem comfortable with the grotesque and I hoped she wasn't taken to lightheadedness. She courteously assured me she was fine but I kept my eye on her.

"No vomiting, diarrhea, coughing, sneezing, excessive thirst, weight loss, problems with breathing?" I ran the list of standard queries trying to keep her talking.

"No, nothing. He even ate his breakfast—somehow—this morning!" She was regaining some of her color.

I was almost finished with my physical exam. Sheila still leaned on the edge of the stainless steel table, now smoothing Nicholas's sides with both of her hands. Her polished nails were perfect tools for scratching her pet's shoulders, though it was difficult for me to hear his heart above his now-symphonic purr.

"Well," I continued, watching Nicholas contently half-squint his eyes, "I'll take him in to suture this back together under an anesthetic. We'll convert it back from a serpent's to a cat's tongue. Hopefully, the sutures will hold, and he'll be as good as new." I acted confident so she would be calm. I worried how straightforward the repair would actually be. Clearly we couldn't leave this the way it was, and I told myself I could only make him better.

"He's happy when the weather's nicer, like the Indian summer we just had. You know, the average temperature during that snap was a full twenty-two degrees warmer than usual for this month. So he was out more than in but I guess that meant more trouble for Nicholas." Sheila knitted her brow slightly as she stroked his forehead. I recognized some connection with her that endeared her to me.

"Maybe you could poke around the barn and see what he got into."

She frowned but nodded in agreement. "Well, this will be a labor of love. That barn's really not the sort of place I'd volunteer to go but I'll see what I can find. Thanks for your help, Dr. Bors. I'll stop by the front desk and get an estimate. This will come out of Nicholas's emergency fund that I hoped I'd never need to use!"

I turned to my patient, "Nicholas Lickolas! That name will suit you! This injury is your little secret, isn't it? Well, I'm going to get you all fixed up, little friend."

He continued to rub, appreciating my attentions. I carried him back to a cage in the small kennel room where he would patiently await that evening's surgery.

As soon as I finished the afternoon's appointments, I gave Nicholas his dose of anesthesia under the skin and kissed him behind his ear. Twenty minutes later, he was immobile and feeling no pain. I studied the jagged, severed edges of Nicholas's disfigured tongue, now eager to correct it. Surely my friend found his condition both painful and less than perfectly functional. Without surgery, one or both halves would quickly shrivel to a token segment.

I sutured a top layer first, then an identical layer on the underside of the tongue. I started at the back of the tear and stitched my way to the tip of the tongue, joining together tiny sections. When the purple suture line reached the tip, the edges joined together perfectly. I hoped I had picked the proper suture type for the job, one that would hold well enough, but then dissolve when the tissue healed. Fortunately, tissues in the mouth tend to heal quickly, I reminded myself, and should be forgiving. I placed him on a cushy towel in his cage.

"Well, Nicholas, let's hope this suits you, buddy. We're going to put you on a special diet for a little while."

He woke slowly and steadily. The next morning, he greedily dived his head into his wet food as if he'd been days without sustenance. Amused, I presumed he felt just fine. Sheila came to collect him. I brought him into an empty exam room and showed her the suture line, which looked great to me, but not to her. She quickly averted her eyes, holding out the palm of her hand.

"And he has such a great personality!" I gushed. "He just seems to have a tremendous outlook on life—everyone's his friend, nothing upsets him and that motor of his is a great way to communicate."

As if he knew we were discussing him, Nicholas sat, chest puffed forward, ears like antennae adjusting to catch the clearest signal.

She responded, "You should hear him purr at home if you think this is loud. I can hear him from upstairs, even if my bedroom door is closed. And you know what else? Every time he hears someone sneeze, he cries."

I laughed, "No way!"

"Yeah, watch." She mustered up a great imitation sneeze. As if on cue, Nicholas perked his ears up. "Meow," he replied, blinking once.

I jumped in, "Let me try! Atchoo!"

He paused. "Meow," he answered laconically, his eyes half closed, the white patch on his neck vibrating to reflect each purr. I was enthralled.

"He's done it ever since he was a kitten," Sheila's eyes sparkled.

When I checked Nicholas again the next week, I stepped into an exam room to find Sheila calmly waiting with him. He was perched on the exam table, front toes just over the edge, orange head held high, an apparent smile on his lips.

"It's Nicholas Lickolas! Have you been staying out of trouble?"

"Well, there's certainly no more drooling. You'd never know there were stitches in there. And he just loves the wet food. He's had twelve cans already, his favorite is the fisherman's platter," she beamed.

I stroked the back of his head and neck, turning on his loud motor. The sutures looked great and healing was underway.

Sheila seemed well matched as a home base for her orange social butterfly. I'd become quite attached to that guy.

Nicholas was back less than two months later, my last appointment of the day.

"Hi, Sheila," I said cheerfully as I entered the exam room. "Though it's a great pleasure, I didn't expect to see you both so soon. What can I do for you today?"

It took Nicholas only a few seconds to command my full attention, lifting his front legs off the exam table as he attained an ultimate rub of his forehead against the palm of my hand.

"Do you mind checking his mouth again? Maybe everything is okay but these last two days, he's dropping his dry food out of his mouth. He still nips at my ankles at five-fifteen every evening to remind me to feed him, so he's still hungry. But I was just hoping you could take a look. I almost peeked, but I chickened out. He'd been doing great all this time!"

I had the uneasy feeling that this was an unexpected repercussion from the original surgery. Did I pick the wrong suture type? Could there be a suture portion left in that was infected or draining? I clucked a soft cat sound near his ear, "t-t-t-t-t," and scratched the top of his head. Carefully opening his lower jaw, I stifled the urge to cry out.

"Sheila, you won't believe this! Nicholas Lickolas has done it again in a new spot! The other area is completely healed. He's split the right quarter of his tongue this time. Do you want to see it?" I talked quickly.

"No thanks."

I smoothed the short hairs between Nicholas's eyebrows, bemused by his relaxed facial expression. "Well, it's a smaller rip this time but still needs stitches or he'll lose that section of the tongue. You know the routine now—I'll do surgery now if he hasn't eaten in a while. Oh, and, by the way, did you ever find any evidence of what he licked?"

"Not a thing! But you should have seen me out there looking, Dr. Bors. You would have been proud of me. I actually tried to follow him out on his round one morning and climbed through brush and bushes and he even led me over to the barn, just like I thought! I felt creepy at first, like I wasn't supposed to be in there, but then it was like a mystery adventure and I was really getting into it. It was even fun getting my sneakers muddy. I lost track of time just seeing where Nicholas hangs out." She was animated as she put a hand on her shoulder and softly smiled.

Sheila kissed Nicholas. "I'll see you tomorrow, Nicholas. You're lucky I love you so much because you've used up your emergency fund and now you're costing me my entire recreational budget." She told me she was an accounting major. It was in her blood, she said. I recognized immediately the value of numbers and discipline to her. Visions of my dear father's gas mileage logs and the frequent nighttime hum of the family adding machine at his organized home desk, him being an accountant for the IRS, ran through my head. Now I knew my connection to Sheila. I had not inherited my dad's joy for balancing figures nor his budget practices. I told her what great company she shared with my dad and that not many college students had their finances so well balanced. Or young veterinarians, I thought, considering my own shoestring lifestyle.

I promised I'd take good care of him and saw Sheila's eyes well up. I lifted Mr. Nicholas into my arms and massaged the fur over his lower backbone, his head lifting toward the ceiling in some ecstatic trance-like state, licking his lips while I scratched.

Nick was preparing to leave for the evening as I readied the anesthesia. Nick jumped when I found him with his head submerged in the hospital cat Spook's cage, murmuring to him as he tucked him in for the night.

"I'm all set back here, Nick," I called. "I'll close up as soon as I'm done. Look who's come to visit again. Remember this cat? Well, he's split his tongue again."

"Fun's fun!" Nick said playfully. "I told you it's the night job around here that gets you. Just when you thought you were gonna get off easy tonight, Dr. B. Wonder what he could have gotten into. Well, call me if you need anything." He leaned the broom back into its proper corner of the kennel room.

"Thanks, Nick. I don't mind with Nicholas—he's named after you, you know."

"Oh, yeah?" His cheeks blushed a little, probably pleased to share such an honor, and he walked through the passageway to the house with the usual cheerful bounce to his step, humming a little tune.

The cat looked at me as if to ask what his next adventure would be. "Nicholas, now I need to have a talk with you, young man." I stroked his back as his motor started up. "You need to start being more discriminating about what you are taste-testing. No more tin cans or whatever it is that you are licking. Do you understand?"

He twitched his right ear slightly, maintaining the posture of a content, self-satisfied individual.

"Oh, what are we going to do with you, Nicholas Lickolas?" I injected his anesthetic dose.

Then I couldn't resist.

"Atchoo! Atchoo!"

Nicholas yawned.

"Meow. . . meow."

# THREE

## *PRINCESS*

On a blustery day like that Tuesday, I decided to wear the new turquoise turtleneck and patterned cable sweater I had just picked up at Hansen's discount store in Plymouth. I shopped there sometimes, buying household supplies and occasional little wardrobe updates. I liked when I found a new sweater on sale like this one for eight dollars. I bought fun new stationery for letters to my dad and my best friend from high school, Stacy. The prices were consumer-friendly enough but there wasn't really anywhere else nearby to go for general goods anyhow. Certainly no malls, so any real fashion shopping waited until a weekend visit to the seacoast where there were malls in Portsmouth and the outlets in Kittery. At the time, I only bought clothes when they were on sale and when I really needed them, my continual quest being the search for the perfect items for work. They needed to both look professional and feel comfy. Since I couldn't fathom plunking down vast amounts of money on one article of clothing that would likely be vomited, urinated or otherwise smeared upon, I stuck to the discount store type, counting on a few pairs of pants, for instance, and interchangeable tops to get me through the week until I could visit the laundromat over the weekend. The strip mall that housed Hansen's also was home to a bank and the one grocery store, P&C, in the area.

Since it seemed he knew most everyone in our town of 1,000 people, Nick rarely made it through his own P&C shopping excursions without running into some of his clients. He did not wish to talk shop when he was in the outside world. That side of his brain he left at the office and that was that, he said. More than once, when picking out Spook's weekly supply of cat food, a client asked his advice on cat food. Nick told me he might as well take on a second job working as a consultant for one of the cat food companies and stand there after hospital hours assisting shoppers. Once when he was in the cereal aisle, someone stopped him to talk about their constipated cat. Another time, when he was at the busy meat counter waiting for his number, a client told Nick in a loud tone how the treatment for his dog's rash just wasn't working and the dog was miserable and Nick would just have to come up with another plan. So Nick adapted an evasive technique to avoid unwanted conversation. Before turning down an aisle, he peeked around each corner and if he spied a person he knew or wished to avoid, he moved quickly ahead to the next row, repeating the process as necessary, then strategically revisited rows he'd skipped.

Nick noticed my new tops and since there were no clients in yet that morning, it was the perfect time to model for him and Becky the new lab coat I'd just ordered and show them how well it fit, with room for my arms to move while still giving my waist some definition. Nick and I made a bet as to how many hours I could keep it clean. I said one day, he said one hour. A can of sardines was riding on this since he and Spook had turned me into a fan of the tasty fishy treats. I was in the midst of a mock runway curtsy and spin when Beth informed Nick and me that we had an emergency headed in, a cat that had been missing for several days. To the owner's distress, the cat came home dragging a leg-hold trap attached to her leg.

Princess and her owner arrived within moments, the cat gingerly packaged in a cardboard box with a thick towel, her right front paw clamped within the jaws of the ugly steel trap. Tears dotted her owner Lynn's eyes as she carried the box to the exam room. How Princess had freed the trap from its stake in the ground was a mystery but she did, its chain dragging behind her. The cat's panicked adrenaline had somehow allowed her to pull the device free, the trap probably not secured properly in the ground in the first place.

"Doctor, I just can't understand it. Thank God she came home. We never would have found her. We'd been searching for her around the neighborhood for days, but we have so many woods behind us, we never would have located her. I didn't know people set traps like this. Is that legal? For God's sake! Oh, I wish I'd never let her be an outdoor cat. It's just that she's so happy when she goes out." Lynn's words streamed one into the other, her anguish punctuating the syllables. "Do you think you can save her leg?" Her tears flowed now, letting go of the stoic facade.

Nick had come into the exam room with me and we gained our bearings. The trap's spring-loaded tines seemed sealed shut around Princess's leg and no amount of brute force would allow us to open it with her awake. How would we open them even when she was asleep, I wondered? Saw them off? I had no idea what we'd do.

I patted the black patch on the cat's head, and she seemed content to lie and allow herself to be tended to. Her eyes were big, black wide-open circles and her appliance dwarfed her petite calico frame. Lynn wrapped her arms around the box for a moment and kissed Princess's forehead.

"Lynn," Nick said, "I've seen something similar a couple other times. I know it's hard to imagine, but most of the time, we salvage the leg. I would hope that this is a soft tissue injury that can heal rather than us needing to amputate. We'll have to see when we remove the trap. We'll give her a sedative so we don't hurt her when it comes off and we'll get some X-rays too, clean that foot up." He looked thoughtful. "When trappers follow the rules, they are supposed to keep their traps a certain distance away from residences to minimize accidental injuries and they are supposed to check their traps daily. The traps are supposed to remain firmly rooted in the ground so an animal doesn't wander off and die with a trap on its leg or get eaten as prey. Fortunately for us, Princess by some miracle did get away and, even more incredibly, found her way back home." I watched the interplay between Lynn and Nick, she hanging on to each of his words, his anger about the poor cat's injury kept hidden from her but I could hear it in his firm words.

She was a lovely cat, brave and smart, I thought. I told Lynn so and touched her shoulder. She smiled a little and said she would wait at home for our call, hoping for good news. Nick carried the box to the X-ray table and I prepared a low dose of anesthesia to give under her skin after listening to her heart. I didn't want to manipulate her any more than we had to. The paw was flattened and quite swollen under the metal. Surely she would need some fluids and antibiotic injections after her ordeal so I prepared those as well.

Nick was affected, I could tell. He hated seeing an animal suffer. He scuffed his shoes and muttered under his breath which I'd come to learn was his way of dealing with anger. I'd never heard him raise his voice, even the time he told the owner of the Nick-sized Great Dane that had tried to maul him that he gave up the zoo practice years ago and could no longer treat her dog—that one was too dangerous. Nick would soon work it out inside himself about Princess, I knew, and for now I said nothing.

How Princess had managed to drag herself home baffled me. Had she chewed at the leg first? Pulled it, yanked it? What had gone through her mind when the trap shut? I wondered if she was panicky or calm. She sure seemed calm now. Maybe it had stopped hurting after a certain point and was now numb. What was she doing anyhow that got her in trouble in the first place? Scouting out a tasty mole somewhere? Sticking her paw into a curious hole?

Nick knew I was too quiet. "Monica, Princess is going to be all right. You'll see." He looked like the gentlest of men just then. I liked his stereotypical image of the kindly, seasoned veterinarian. "You watch. I've actually seen a few of these trap injuries since I've been up here. So far, most of them had soft tissue injuries without broken bones. Now you tell me when Princess is sedate and I'll come back and show you how to take this contraption off."

In a few minutes, Princess was asleep. I alerted Nick and he came back as soon as he finished his appointment. Within moments, her leg was freed. In a motion like opening the front and back covers of a book, with Princess' foot the pages inside, Nick used his strength to pry apart the metallic arms while I slid her paw out.

The swollen paw was double in size and cold to the touch. Flattened sideways, the puffy edema created a grotesque distortion.

"Nick, there is no way that the entire set of carpal bones isn't crushed there! Look at it." I turned to him, cupping the paw in the palm of my hand. "Poor thing." I quieted my emotion.

"Well, let's get that X-ray done. I'll develop it while you soak the foot."

I heard Nick whistling on the other side of the door in the small room with the X-ray developing fluids. We used sequential narrow chemical tanks to dip the films, which were sensitive to temperature changes. Proper timing was important during the process for the films to develop correctly. Nick loved his time away from the fast pace at the office doing just that—nothing but waiting for the next dip. Five minutes when no one would disturb him. When it was my turn to process films, I put them in and slipped out of the room for the next few minutes, impatiently using every moment until I had to change the film hanger into the next vat. I had asked him a few times about getting one of the automatic processors that were the latest and greatest. Keith had one at his practice, and, with it, processing was much less involved. The films were more consistent and the temperature fluctuations controlled. And employees were exposed to fewer open chemicals. Nick agreed about its value but for the time, this was how he chose to continue, this system's nicest benefit being his mental health breaks. Tunes I heard him whistle from the other side of the door on different days ran the gamut from Beethoven's "Ode To Joy" to Elvis's "Burning Love."

As she slept, I wrapped Princess in the thickest towel we had. In a bowl by the sink, I made up a soak solution for her foot. "Princess, you are such a little peanut. How did you get home?" Administering a fluid bolus under her skin, I spoke to the sleeping cat in amazement about her will to endure.

Nick swung open the dark brown door to the developing room, his eyes squinting as he adjusted back to the light. "Hey, Dr. B, they're still wet, but let's hold the films up to the window and see. When they're dry, we can double-check 'em on the view screen."

There was not a displaced bone, no crushes and no fractures, just soft tissue swelling that we could appreciate on the films. "Nick, how did you know? There's no way I would have predicted that. But what about the loss of circulation over time? Won't her toes become gangrenous and still need an amputation? All that swelling and pressure. There's an indent on both sides in the shape of that blasted metal."

"Let's give it a week or so before we make any judgments. We don't have to decide that today. You can have Lynn bring in Princess every couple of days so you can watch what's happening. That way, the cat can be back home where she loves to be and I know Lynn will spoil her rotten. If we have to amputate, we'll also know that as the days go on. Just keep her on her those medications for edema and infection."

Lynn joyfully received the news that Princess would be going home with her that night and that there was a chance that she would come out on the other side of this no worse for the wear, though as I spoke Nick's experienced words of hope, my faith was shaky here. I told her how much I wanted this to heal, as Nick predicted, but also warned her of the other possibility. I was pleased to hand Lynn her precious bundle back in the box, this time lighter. Princess's groggy head rested on top of the folds of her towel and I told her what a brave cat she'd been. I could feel a tiny purr starting under her neck.

Lynn hugged me. "Thanks so much for getting her out of this. You can get rid of the trap for me. I don't ever want to see it again as long as I live." Nick had informed us that trappers were supposed to label their devices but this one bore no identification. I told her to double up on the loving for Princess as I was sure she would. The way the room light caught her hair, I noticed that the black in Princess's fur pattern was the same pretty color as Lynn's hair. I pointed that out to her and we joked that she could further coordinate the look next time with an orange sweater and white pants.

The rest of that day stayed busy for Nick and me and I was tired at the end. When I hung my new lab coat on the hook, Nick observed a stain on the lower front pocket area.

"Ha!" he said, "And did you think you were going to hide that blemish on your coat from me? Pretty sneaky if you ask me, Dr. B. And precisely when did you acquire that?" His soft chuckle brightened my mood.

I looked down at the corner of my coat and saw the reddish brown colored smear. "I never noticed that, Nick. I wonder what it is. I probably just earned it and so I'd be the winner, as now is closer in work hours to tomorrow than it is to this morning," I reasoned.

"That looks like rust to me. How on earth . . .? I've got it. That trap. I bet you rubbed into it when you were taking care of Princess. And that was this morning. In fact, it was probably within the first hour. So I win. I'll give you a week's grace period on the sardines—King Oscar, in mustard, of course. My favorite."

"Darn, and I thought surely I would get this one. Okay, okay, but one of these times . . ." I shook my head as I pulled on my jacket and gloves. He always seemed to win these things lately.

As I lay in bed that night, images of Princess in the woods and other potential vulnerable creatures springing the trap kept me awake. Even when I tried to think of other things, I was awake. Somehow Nick had found a way to distance himself from the personal distress aspect of his work while maintaining his empathy and compassion for our patients. I supposed it was a fine line that he walked well, one that I was yet to learn. When sleep finally came, I dreamed that someone bound and gagged me and I woke up anxious. Seeing Moosehead on my bedcovers helped me shake off my nightmare, though the mood stuck and I wondered if my personality would allow me ever to get to the point where work stayed at work without me losing my connection to my cases. How did pediatric neurosurgeons steel themselves enough to do their jobs? Did they bring it home with them? How about oncologists? How did they control their own fear for their patients' survival and still negotiate the mountain they were attempting to conquer?

I examined Princess the next day and found that her foot was indeed warm. It was still as swollen but there was circulation. Lynn said Princess devoured the chicken she cooked her and she slept on the bed since she'd been home. "Oh, little one, you must have been exhausted." I stroked her back between her shoulders and lightly examined her toes. How fantastic to see the light pink pads. Princess squirmed and mewed a soft sound and when the rectal thermometer came out, I had Beth help hold her by her scruff. It was good to know she had feeling in the foot and equally as good to glimpse a spirited side to her. Lynn indicated that this was more usual for Princess at the vet's office than the quiet demeanor we had previously seen. Surely she was healing. Whispers of relief worked their way into my ears.

Nick had accurately predicted the course and I was grateful for his guidance. In fact, Princess made a remarkable recovery. Over the days, the swelling declined steadily and Princess used the foot when she walked around at home. Lynn regularly brought us treats with her visits, donuts from the Java Hut and cookies she had baked.

Every time Princess arrived, she held her head proud and alert. She allowed me to pat the black mask on the top of her head that surrounded her ears and cheeks, where I sometimes earned a little purr but the white patch on the sides of her neck and shoulders was not to be touched. She had become wise to injections where we scruffed her on the loose folds of skin at the back of the neck, the place momma cats carry their kittens. For cats that felt misunderstood at the office and acted out, holding the scruff was a basic and important restraint technique for their safety and ours. Princess acted hot and cold, sometimes sweet and lovable but other times I crossed the line with her. The healing was far enough along that it was no longer necessary to set her off with the thermometer and for the most part, we kept the rechecks pleasant and quick. Each time, I felt us further away from danger. Her long-term prognosis, in fact, was now excellent.

This one would be our last visit, as all seemed well. She was a magnificent feline sitting in the new wicker cat basket Lynn had bought at Hansen's. She took right to it as soon as it came home, Lynn said. Lynn picked out one with a yellow pillow to best complement the yellowy-orange on Princess' front legs.

"Doctor Bors, thank you so much," Lynn was warm and sincere. "I brought you something I saw that I hoped you would like. You don't know how much all your care and Dr. Schatzle's kindness and Beth at this hospital have helped me deal with her injury. I've felt so terrible about this. It's hard to stop thinking about what it was like for her, but anyhow, it's such a relief that she is better. She'll stay inside from now on."

I received the gift she had wrapped in tissue paper. I exclaimed as I unfolded a new scrub top, livened with images of comical cats in various stages of play.

"Lynn, this is great! Where did you ever find it? And just my size!" I could see Beth peek around the corner of the door as I slipped the new shirt over my head.

"Well, let's just say it was a co-conspiracy and that Beth is a good source of information," Lynn winked.

Princess lounged on her pillow, her front half sitting up, her back half leaning on her left hip. A lazy tail hung off the edge of the basket. This clever girl rested her shoulder against the high back of the basket, a queen's dispensation to her subjects evident in the confident narrowing of the now-pleased green eyes. Both front paws grandly bore Princess' weight, both equal in size.

# FOUR

## *DUSTY*

"Oh, please let this one be something different," I groaned to myself as I lifted the next record out of its slot in the exam room door.

Monthly vaccine reminder postcards must have just been mailed out. Beth filled them in by hand as patients were in for their annual visits. She kept them in an organized file to be mailed out a month prior to the next year's due date. They were batched monthly and the phones rang heartily for a couple days after with appointments heavily stacked. Anyone who hadn't had a heartworm blood test yet in the spring got caught up there as well. This made for busy few days each, with most appointments seen being near-repeats of the ones before.

As I looked at the record, I found I'd gotten what I wanted: "Check over—losing weight." Good. An interesting case that would allow me to use my investigative skills to hopefully help the animal waiting in the room. The record revealed that this was the first time this twelve-year-old dog had been to our hospital.

I caught my breath as I entered the room. The small blond shepherd-terrier mix on the stainless steel exam room table was a mass of skin-draped bones and her respiratory efforts were exaggerated. She lay prone, unwilling or unable to raise her head. No mere weight loss problem, I quickly assessed.

"Hi, I'm Dr. Bors." I greeted the owner and directly turned my attention to the dog. A wave of anger flushed through me as I wondered how anyone could have let their animal get in this condition without seeking medical treatment. I quieted my emotion and proceeded.

"Wow, Mrs. Gentry, what's going on with Dusty here? I see she's quite thin—how long's she been like this?"

Her owner, a slender, severe woman, pulled her small frame up squarely. I noticed the perfectly pressed lapels on her crisp frock and how they matched the pale yellow of the room's walls.

"Dusty just isn't herself today." She spoke brusquely. "She's been eating a little less each day and has been less active but I've been doing a lot of nursing care on her myself at home. I'm trained as a nurse and I know how to take care of these things. I just thought I'd reached the point where I should have someone take a look at her. Maybe there's something you can give her."

The helpless dog was too weak to walk on her own. Dusty was clearly dehydrated, her chest sounded raspy, and her abdomen felt empty of either food or feces. Her body temperature was too low, never a good sign. It would be cruel to let her go on like this, having reached this point of emaciation and indignity. We would have to do something one way or another. Surely the owner would agree. I took a deep breath.

"Dusty's very sick, Mrs. Gentry. While I can't tell you by her physical exam alone exactly what disease she has, she looks to me as though she's suffering. See her lack of muscle mass? She's broken down most of her body stores of energy. I suspect she has liver or kidney failure, or even cancer, although there are a lot of other diseases that could cause her condition. Now, we could go one of two routes. I could do some blood tests and X-rays to find out what is wrong, then hospitalize her to start her on IV fluids and other medications to see if we can help her. Honestly, though, I think the kindest thing would be to put her to sleep today."

She blinked once. The fine lines that circled her mouth barely moved as she spoke. "No. That's not what I came here for. I'm not ready for her to die yet and I don't want any tests done on her. I won't let her be hospitalized. I just want you to give me something to help her out until she dies."

I hesitated. Many owners agonize over this decision in the earlier stages of their pets' downturn, some seeking validation that this was indeed the right thing to do. There was no question in my mind about what was fair for Dusty now. Home care just didn't seem like an option.

"Without knowing exactly what is wrong with her, it would be a guess which medications to use. It would all just be supportive stuff, like a nutrient supplement paste and antibiotics. However, she looks like she's going to continue to struggle until the very end. I really think we should put her to sleep now, and, if not that, at least hospitalize her to efficiently get her some intravenous fluids. There's no middle road with her."

"Well, that is your opinion, doctor. It is not mine. What I want is for you to give me the medicines you mentioned so that I can continue taking care of her at home."

My face was flushing. I'd have to avoid stumbling over my words as I answered her. Maybe she really didn't understand how far gone Dusty was. I had tried to withhold any judgment from my tone while remaining a strong advocate for Dusty. It wasn't easy for me to recommend euthanasia and I never made that recommendation lightly. In fact, this was one of the hardest parts of the job for me as a veterinarian. Experiencing that moment from life to death and needing to sometimes steel myself away from the emotion-packed moments. Feeling the gravity of the decision. Being certain beyond doubt in some cases that this was the right thing to do, sharing with owners the deep privilege of being with them in the leaving of their beloved pet's spirit. Crying together. There were sometimes nightmares, particularly after weeks with several euthanasia procedures. In one, I was named "Euthanasia Doctor of the Year." I had shared deeply the poignant sadness of many families undergoing the loss associated with their pets' terminal illness. As well, I still struggled with my feelings about some of the less obvious cases—cases in which I truly felt we could help the animal with therapy that the owner chose not to pursue or times when a healthy but badly tempered animal was at issue. In the situation before me, however, I bore no ambivalence. Mrs.

Gentry's motivations remained a mystery to me. Could she be in denial? Perhaps the owner was unwilling to spend money on the vet bills. Or maybe she felt it would be a failing of her nurturing skills if Dusty died. Based on the tone and words she had spoken to me so far, I wondered most whether she wanted to control this situation, including her dog's death.

"Look, I can't force you to have Dusty euthanized or hospitalized. If you're going to try home care, you need to be bolstering her fluid and calorie intake. Now she's not vomiting and there's no diarrhea, right?"

"Right." She did not look in my eyes or even at my face as I tried to look into hers.

If she insisted on her type of care, I wanted to be sure she worked hard to support this dog's last few days. Explicit instructions were mapped out with Mrs. Gentry—dribbling a rehydrating electrolyte drink made for children into her mouth eight to ten times a day, spoon-feeding pureed meats or baby food six times a day, turning Dusty over several times a day and padding her bedding to avoid sores and charting her progress.

"You have to promise to do these things for her. Also that you'll call the office with updates."

"Well, yes . . . of course." She lightened a bit.

"And, for her sake, if her breathing becomes labored—basically anything worse than it is now—you'll need to bring her in to be put to sleep."

"If I'm ready."

"Mrs. Gentry, this is a time when you have to think of Dusty, not of your still wanting to hold on to her." I tried to say the words gently. The room felt suddenly hot. I hoped my outer professional demeanor did not betray my inner dislike for this woman. I knew I was not projecting the same affection I usually shared with my patients' owners, but I couldn't help it in this case.

"I know my dog a lot better than you do and it's not time yet. I watched my mother die at home when I was sixteen years old. *I* was the one who took care of her needs. I know what to do and certainly know what *my* dog needs." She stood straight up again, her chin slightly raised so that her tidy chignon just brushed the back of her neck.

My words had clearly offended her. I couldn't alienate her for Dusty's sake. To me, it seemed so clear that when an animal could no longer eat and drink well enough to nourish her body, was unable to walk or attend to her own bathroom needs, was working to breathe, had no hopes of recovery and had lost her dignity and pride, it was time to make this decision. Any one of these reasons was usually enough to warrant discussions about euthanasia.

"Well, listen, we need to be working together here." I tried to recover. "I would love to be wrong and see her pull through this, but . . . she's just so sick. You need to keep her as comfortable as we can."

A short silence lay heavy in the air. Mrs. Gentry looked briefly at me, her eyes squinted, then toward the window.

"If she's going to die, I just want her to die at home with me there." Her tone was firm. "Why can't you just give me a pill I can give her at home—like an overdose or something that will make her die in her sleep?"

I paused to pick my words.

"No . . . the only humane way is by intravenous injection. It's quick and painless and just makes her sleep. Then the drug takes her deeper to stop the brain and heart. There are no pills I can give you to do that at home."

"But there are some made that would do the job."

"No . . . I didn't say that. I wouldn't even know what they would be nor would I prescribe them. It's wrong."

"What if *I* found out the drug you need and the dose?"

I brushed the bangs off my forehead. I wondered if I was developing an ulcer. Two deep breaths. "No."

"I want a tranquilizer for her then. Enough to get her through for a while." She continued on.

"She doesn't need a tranquilizer. Look, call us back on Monday and tell us how you are doing getting the fluid and slurried food into her—like I said, many times a day."

With that, I ended the exasperating office call far behind schedule. I hoped the rest were all routine visits.

Monday came and went without my hearing from Mrs. Gentry. I figured Dusty had probably died at home and I didn't relish the idea of calling to find out. Tuesday morning, Beth informed me that Mrs.

Gentry wanted a call back. She was short with Beth and wouldn't leave a message.

I felt it important for me to move beyond my judgments of her and soften for her as I would anyone else. I called at my first free moment. "Mrs. Gentry, this is Dr. Bors. How is Dusty?"

"Well I think she's doing a little bit better." Her businesslike tone did not waver.

"Oh, really?!? That's great. Is she taking in the fluid and food?"

I pictured Dusty's forced feedings, the slurried mash and electrolyte solution, the towel to wipe her muzzle, which Mrs. Gentry reported she was feeding every two hours during the day and once during the night. She described carrying the dog to the yard, where Dusty would briefly stand. She was keeping a log book of Dusty's breathing rate, taken three times a day. Maybe we could use her nursing training to help us gauge Dusty's progress or lack of it. Maybe her seeing it on paper . . .

Against my predictions, Dusty did not rapidly take a turn for the worse. She lingered, still not able to get up and walk around on her own. She apparently plateaued at a level slightly better than the day I first examined her. I could not be sure because I had to rely on over-the-phone assessments, since Mrs. Gentry would not bring the dog back in. She did report every few days on the progress of Dusty's respiratory rates, never leaving a message at the front desk, insisting on speaking to me only. I never enjoyed these calls and she was not warm on the phone, despite my efforts to draw her out, to find out something about her that we could connect on. She was the one who often abruptly decided that the phone call was over and that was that. Dusty's feeding and fluid regimen continued. The palliative effect of the antibiotics and nutrition seemed to be keeping Dusty's body in this limbo state.

Two weeks later, the routine was on going. Several times I asked Mrs. Gentry to let me examine Dusty and as many times, she refused. When I visited the subject of euthanasia, I was firmly informed by Mrs. Gentry that she wasn't ready.

Financially, the owner had managed to achieve a real bargain. One office call charge and initial medications and by being difficult most times to the receptionist, she had my rapt attention for free on the phone several times a week. Why had I let things get this way? I reminded myself

I was Dusty's agent when she needed someone standing up for her. But even here, I wasn't sure I was helping her, even though it was out of my hands what the owner chose to do. I couldn't force her to come in. While the feedings kept Dusty's existence a bit more comfortable, I waited for a change in Mrs. Gentry's attitude—for Dusty's sake.

In a way, some peace did eventually settle into my mind. I had learned to put the Gentry family out of my thoughts as I lay in bed at night and realized that this was their decision; I could not control this. As weary as the case made me, I had done as much as I knew to do.

One night, almost three weeks after I had first examined Dusty, I was the doctor on call. My telephone had been silent all night and so I slept a deep, dreamless sleep. Until she called.

"Dr. Bors? It's time now."

"Excuse me?" I couldn't figure where I was.

"This is Arlene Gentry. Dusty—it's time for her to be put to sleep."

The glow of the digital numbers on my clock radio taunted me with its 1:04 a.m. readout. After all these weeks when I had spoken with her in the middle of the day, dressed and ready to work, at the office.

Nick would have refused if it had been his case. He wouldn't have let it get so far out of hand in the first place. Maybe he would have been able to convince Mrs. Gentry the first day to do the right thing. He wouldn't have let her direct everything the way she had. Not only did I feel that I had failed the dog, but I felt completely taken advantage of.

"Mrs. Gentry, can't this wait until the morning? I'll be in the office at seven." My annoyance woke me up. I propped up on one elbow.

"No . . . I really think she's suffering now. She's having trouble breathing. You're not going to make poor Dusty suffer through the night, are you?" I felt the dagger twist in my heart.

My language came in controlled single syllables.

"I'll be right in." My room was cold and the thought of bundling to head down the hill to work was not welcome.

"Oh . . . can you wait thirty minutes to get there so my son can be there too? He gets off of work at McDonald's in fifteen minutes." Was I still groggy or did she actually sound cheery?

"No. I will either come in right now or it will wait until seven a.m."

"All right—I'll head in now."

I lived about twelve or fifteen minutes from the practice depending on if the road was icy. I knew she lived twenty minutes away. I got up and made myself a quick bowl of cereal. Not happy. No instant coffee or I'd never get back to sleep when I returned home. I pulled on my coat, hat and gloves and trudged out the door.

When I arrived at the hospital, Mrs. Gentry was not there yet. I sat at the reception desk flipping the pages of the appointment book back and forth, memorizing the schedule for the next few days. Beth had already pulled out the files that would be coming in the next day and they were in a tidy pile by the telephone. I put my head down to rest. Twenty more minutes passed before a car pulled up. Finally, I thought. It had been thirty-five minutes since she called me. My eyes were bleary, my bed beckoned and besides, it was the principle of the whole thing. At least I could put the suffering dog at peace, I told myself.

It wasn't Mrs. Gentry who walked in the door, it was her teenage son in his McDonald's uniform. She had stalled anyhow. Another car pulled into the hospital's driveway momentarily. Instead of Mrs. Gentry, it was a young woman, her daughter. Had she been a willing witness or had she too been a victim of manipulation? Then a third vehicle. Mr. and Mrs. Gentry arrived with the dog. Mr. Gentry remained silent as his thick arms carried the immobile Dusty. On the exam table, Dusty's labored breathing was obvious, her body condition as poor as before except now she sported a large circular bedsore on her right hip.

The family gathered in this surreal scene around Dusty. I had no words. My focus was completely on Dusty.

"Sweetheart, this will be over soon and you can rest—no more struggling." I spoke softly and stroked her under her chin. Her soulful eyes locked into mine. Mine welled in tears, not for what was soon to be, but for my utter frustration about what this sweet dog had to endure this past month. *Forgive us human beings.* I hoped to transmit my thoughts to Dusty. I quickly gathered myself—I could let myself cry later but not in front of Mrs. Gentry.

I administered the slow injection of euthanasia solution into Dusty's vein. Within seconds, her muscles relaxed completely as she laid her head on its side on the table. Her breathing slowed, then stopped. I listened for a heartbeat—there was none.

"She's gone," I said quietly, not looking up.

No one in the room spoke. Perhaps they too would cry later. The family had decided to bury her at home, since the ground was thawed, so they would take her back home.

As we reached the front desk, I told Mrs. Gentry she needed to pay for the emergency office call that night. I had the feeling that "out of sight" would mean "outstanding balance" with this owner.

"Oh, I didn't bring any money with me, this being such an emergency and all."

"How about a credit card or a check?"

"No . . . I left the checkbook at home in all the confusion and I don't have a charge card." It was the only time I'd seen her crack a smile, albeit a sheepish one.

"I do, Mother." The daughter spoke up, a look of exasperation on her face that was a younger, pretty version of her mother's.

"Thank you," I said, looking only at the daughter. I completed the transaction, and handed her the card back.

"Doctor, thank you for your efforts . . ." The young woman looked into my eyes, then back at her mother across the room and then she looked down and spoke quietly, "my mom, she's . . . I'm sorry . . ." She focused on the floor as she left the hospital.

"Well, see, we've done Dusty a great favor," Mrs. Gentry, across the room, spoke proudly to her son, holding her shoulders square, as she too moved out the door.

Home in bed, I never fell back asleep. My clock radio blinked 3:17, 3:17, 3:18. My dreamless night would continue. Could've had that instant coffee after all.

# FIVE

## *JOB BENEFITS*

My job had the kind of benefits not written into any contract. Like the scales of justice, these balanced out the hard parts. Life was full and the stress level could easily topple into the dangerous range. However, there has been no other time in my life where I was so molded by such goodness both in people and in my surroundings.

For one, Nick, Beth and I delighted in the antics of Nick's mostly black cat, Spook, who lived in the clinic. At night, Spook slept in a cage in the kennel room, tucked in with his special brown blanket on which he snuggled the white parts of his front paws under his breastbone. By day, after he'd eaten breakfast, Spook entertained his guests, nonchalantly strolling through the waiting room making sure all felt welcome. It wasn't unusual for me to step out of an exam room and find Spook curled up on a pet owner's lap or calmly rubbing his body along the side of a sick dog that was resting in the waiting room, ministering to it. Spook toured the hospital grounds, sometimes sitting on a client's car hood, refusing to budge even when it was time for the person to leave. More than once, he waited inside a client's car, having jumped in an open window, ready to accompany the family home for an exciting adventure. He ate anything he was offered including what was left over in the bowls of our hospitalized patients. Beth taught me the habit of closing the empty cage doors while our patient was out for treatment or else we found Spook inside, enjoying some extra morsels. We placed the food dishes of our patients toward the back of their cages since Spook sometimes reached his arm inside the bars of the closed door to try to scoop out a snack. Though Nick kept Spook on a diet, he occasionally treated him to some of his beloved King Oscar sardines, quickly devoured by a grateful feline.

Nick was just what I needed—a gentle, guiding hand and a great example, all the while allowing me to develop my own style. Nick modeled for me a unique sensitivity for owners and their pets and they clearly appreciated him. He could just as easily act goofy enough to pacify an overtired toddler and her overstressed mother as he could diagnose the cause of their exuberant dog's knee injury. Without putting himself behind in the appointment schedule, Nick and Alvie Gordon shared spirited discourse about Doug Flutie's crossing the picket line for the Patriots during the NFL players' strike, all while examining and administering vaccines to Alvie's golden retriever Ben. When Meryl Potter's boxer jumped through a plate glass window because of a severe thunderstorm anxiety, he calmed Meryl's distress while we prepared to suture the dog's multiple lacerations. His client greetings in the waiting room were warm and genuine. At least four clients proudly claimed their animal was Nick's very first patient when he opened the Norwich clinic and was working out of his garage. Nick always laughed when I informed him I just met another one of his "very first" patients. People trusted his word and trusted their animals utterly in his hands.

His even temperament never took to moodiness. Beth and I could daily count on Nick's cheerful greeting, upbeat attitude and mugs of hot instant coffee he brought over from the house for us just before the day's appointments began. He usually slipped over to the house for a few moments after the cleaning chores and treatments were completed, the teakettle heated for him. That quick visit with Gail was good for his spirits as he arrived back neatened and relaxed. Over the top of my mug, he considerately placed a piece of paper to keep it from cooling before I had a chance to drink it, as he knew I was usually distracted from finishing all but a few sips right away.

One morning Nick came back to the clinic wearing a newly laundered lab coat fresh from the dryer. As he readied for our appointments, I was absorbed in my evaluation of a blood smear in our small laboratory. I heard Nick greet the first client and usher her to the exam room. I looked up as Nick entered the room behind the pet owner, in time to notice an artifact of static cling attached to the back of his clean lab jacket. No ordinary item was this, though. It was a pair of Gail's underwear and I was one hundred percent certain that she would not appreciate Nick walking around with that on his back. But how to proceed, I wondered, since he had just closed that room door, unaware. Knock and say, "Excuse me, Nick, there's a pair of underwear on your back?" Hope he doesn't turn his back on the patient and that it doesn't fall on the floor? Even if I did nothing and it stayed on his back, what would the owner think when she saw it? And if it did land on the floor, Nick would have absolutely no idea where that had just come from, as if it had just descended from the sky or his client had dropped it from her purse. As it was, I entered the room under the guise of needing a supply and casually placed my hand on his back, then delivered the item to my own pocket in a swift maneuver that would make most shoplifters proud. The pet owner was none the wiser. When Nick came out of the room, Beth's and my eyes were rimmed with tears from the laughter we'd just recovered from. I showed him what was in my pocket as soon as the clinic was empty and he was bewildered, which sent Beth and me into another spasm. I had enough fuel to tease Nick for the entire next week. Gail, of course, was mortified but when she realized that no clients were privy to the item, she let ring her hearty laugh that always made me feel all was right in the world.

It was great fun around the office to collect as many client-derived malapropisms of Nick's and my last names as we could. Nick clearly held the record. My Dr. Bors became Dr. Board, Dr. Boris, Dr. Morris and The Lady Doctor. Dr. Schatzle, however, was transformed to the more flavorful Dr. Schatzie, Dr. Schlitz, Dr. Shackle, Dr. Schlotz, Dr. Schwatzle, Dr. Shultzie, Dr. Schnitzle and even Dr. Schnauzer, to name a few. We took to addressing each other in the form of the latest inaccuracy of the day, Beth leading the charge.

There was mirth. Nick's round face shined when he was happy and the top of his fair cheeks blushed pink. His shoulders rose and fell when he laughed, his body still in control while he chuckled. It made me laugh more just watching him. Nick stood a bit taller than me, and his close-cut, prematurely gray hair added an air of distinction. More than one female client had expressed to me a wish that Nick was single but he was happily married to his fashionable and lovely wife Gail.

Nick and Gail were well matched. She was kind and hospitable, having cooked me a Thanksgiving-type meal when I first interviewed and having helped me scout out housing when I first moved to Norwich. They opened their home to me at all times, inviting me to stay there when they were away, which I did. That privilege served me well during a snowy cold snap. I brought Amos and Moosehead to board at the clinic for a few days once when Gail and Nick took a southern vacation and, after work ended, parked myself in front of their kitchen wood stove and settled into the billowy reading chair beneath a blanket, lit from a pull-string standing lamp. I had brought into the house with me a formerly stray Springer spaniel cross we called Mitzi that was staying at the hospital for a few days, nursing a leg wound and soon to be adopted, but for now she had only us. I was in love with her and she sweetly drank in my attentions, curled at my feet while I sat, watching my face for directions. How I wished she could be mine, so very loyal and clever a girl but the time was not now with my schedule and, besides, a new owner was found who had acreage and more time. At night I slept in the Schatzle's luxurious queen-sized guest bed with an overstuffed comforter and featherbed and come morning, stepped my toes onto the antique wooden floor. Breakfast in their generous kitchen was eaten seated on the puffy, patterned pillows on the bar stools arranged around the kitchen island. Gail had left me fresh bagels and English muffins with cream cheeses flavored with hazelnut and strawberry. I enjoyed the morning news on the little kitchen television while I ate, a treat, barely able to fathom what gumption it must take to daily measure the perverse wind speeds atop Mount Washington that the meteorologists reported. The woodstove scent and warmth bathed my senses. Now I understood the magic of Nick's peaceful place to which he escaped whenever he could.

The genius of Nick's clinic design was its simplicity. The longitudinal layout made for an easy and natural flow—two exam rooms on the right hand side of the hallway, which led to the wide treatment and surgery area, and then the large kennel room and outdoor runs. Nick utilized the raised bathtub in the kennel room every day since every patient that stayed overnight was bathed the next morning. All went home clean and shiny, as Nick said, his "calling card."

Nick's building suited him just right, no fancy modern suites necessary. He had designed the two unique exam room tables to be bolted flush along one wall, with no supporting legs to get in the way. Each table bore a hook and a light metal chain at one end, these also bolted into the wall. I was amazed at how calm a nervous dog or cat became if the chain was gently placed around its neck like a leash, like a signal for them to behave cooperatively. I do believe that this setup was part of Nick's secret of autonomy, since many procedures, even drawing blood, became possible to perform without an assistant.

From work each evening on my way out the door, Nick told me, "Thank you for all your good help today," his eyes twinkling, and he really meant it. When there were workups to do after appointments, he'd comment, "It's not the day job, it's the night job around here that kills me," a line that summed it all up and one I came to store in my satchel of phraseology, a way to simultaneously whine with levity, yet feel validated for being annoyed. We'd be finished seeing patients at six in the evening only to have collected a couple of cat abscesses that needed lancing and suturing and perhaps a medical case that required X-rays, blood work, fluids and such. Usually, we both stayed to help each other when we could, cutting down the burden. "We're a team, you know, Dr. B. None of this lone rider stuff," he said when I insisted the dinner Gail cooked him must be getting cold. Nick divided our duties "fair and square . . . you just let me know if there's something you think isn't fair."

On the other hand, it wasn't all fun and games. There was reality. The on-call duty was a heavy burden of responsibility to me. Making the right decisions alone about what to do when I didn't already have the answer or the experience drove my anxiety into the stratosphere. I hated the trip back to the hospital during the night. Nick fortunately didn't have far to go when emergencies rang and, for him, having been on duty seven nights a week for the ten years prior to my joining him, it must have been a great relief to cut his times in half and for that I was happy to be there. He didn't care for beepers, and he was certain the town's telephone technology wasn't supportive of them anyhow—the time warp allowed us only one phone line and rotary dial, so I was tied to my home phone half the week. This required the people who I shared a house with to keep their calls short as well. My stress load was increased because there was no veterinary technician on staff. Nick was so self-sufficient that he rarely needed Beth to help hold animals while administering anesthesia or other treatments. While the extra duties were routine and many of them enjoyable for Nick, I saw this as time and energy taken away from my veterinary tasks. We took and developed all our own X-rays, ran all our in-house blood work, did all the treatments, connected the IV's, sterilized the surgical packs, cleaned cages, bathed animals and shared in the hospital cleaning in addition to keeping up with appointments and surgery. Of course, Beth was very busy tending the front desk, keeping appointments running smoothly, answering phones, prioritizing the emergency calls, checking clients in and out, tallying the books and keeping Nick and me in line.

We each worked a five-day week and alternated weekends off. Whoever was on duty for the weekend saw the scheduled Saturday appointments and was usually finished by one in the afternoon unless any emergencies came in. Most of the difficult hours were simply a result of the realities of life in a small, rural town. Some of our clients from other towns traveled forty-five minutes to the office, since we were the closest veterinary hospital to several parts of the White Mountain region. There were no emergency clinics to turn over calls to, so we took all our own, splitting the week between the two of us. While it was a busy existence, the trade-off was the pure way of life, the ever beautiful surroundings and the opportunity to be nurtured by such a kind advisor as Nick. I would forever bear the softest of spots in my heart for him, my mentor, and vowed to stay connected to him and Gail no matter what.

# SIX

## *CHARMAINE*

Some dogs were big enough that they were best examined on the floor. Alex was one such friend. This proud, docile Doberman led his mistress Darryl to the exam room where I stood. He readily filled the room with his broad chest, full body and wiggling stub of a tail. Darryl encouraged Alex's affectionate nuzzling and they both greeted me enthusiastically. The dog glistened where melted snowflakes had covered his black fur. Darryl slid off her fuzzy white hat, it also dewy.

"Good morning, Dr. Bors. How are you liking this string of storms? Seems we get them every February. Isn't everything so pristine and unspoiled?"

I playfully thumped Alex's chest with both hands as I leaned over him. "I was just thinking it was time for winter to go away! I have a hard time getting comfortable in the cold season. But I do admit, you're right. It is stunning to see the town common and the old church steeple covered and the tree branches heavy and low like over our driveway here. People say the key is to have a sport you can enjoy, so I'm trying on these trails and fields." I told her about my cross-country skiing attempts.

Alex nudged the corner of my lab coat pocket where surely he detected some remaining dog cookie crumbs. I slipped him a fresh one from my stash in the top drawer of the table.

"I'm invigorated by it. You should see my horse these days, flipping her mane, prancing around so proud. . . totally in her element. And Alex, he's a clown in the snow, jumping and rolling." Darryl's face was kind and warm. She spoke with the hint of a Southern drawl, which was enigmatic to me up here in the mountains of New Hampshire.

While we talked about how much we both loved Dobies and how they were most often trustworthy sweethearts when raised right, Alex leaned his shoulder into my legs for maximum contact, turning his face upward in a sideways grin of sorts. I felt his lean abdomen and deep chest, listened to his heart and checked over his face and body. I hoped that he simply perceived my exam as a full body massage. It was as I administered his second vaccine that a swath of melancholy fazed me. The casual tilt of Darryl's head as she recounted Alex's eating habits caught me up short. There was a familiarity for me there, a fondness, a trigger. My mind pulled me back two years. One of my closest friends in veterinary school had once owned a Doberman that she rescued and dearly loved, but Iver loved only her. Fiercely protective of Char and constantly at her side, he was nicknamed Devil Dog by the rest of her family.

I shook my head, clearing my mind to focus. *Let me finish this appointment with this nice lady and lovely dog*, I thought. I forced a smile and it was soon time to escort them both to the front desk. We exchanged pleasantries as Darryl adjusted her cap onto her pretty shoulder-length hair and pulled on her parka.

Lunchtime came next and I slipped into the small office room to eat last night's leftovers from my bag. Nick was away that day, so I'd be better off to take a low-key lunch at the office just in case an animal emergency arose. I preferred to stay off the road in active weather anyhow. Sometimes I drove around after stopping at my post office box at lunchtime but not today. I studied the calendar and realized that in three days it would be February 11. Darn it. Maybe a card would still get to her parents on time. I could use one from the box of blank cards Nick kept on the shelf at the office. I propped my head on my folded arms on the desk, wide-awake, pensive.

I don't specifically remember meeting Charmaine but just like that, she was in my life and it was as if I'd always known her. We simply gravitated toward one another that beginning year of veterinary school. I was attracted by her easy smile and infectious laugh. Being idealistic freshman together, neither of us curve-breakers, we struggled through anatomy exams and shared similar goals and ideals.

Two nights before our first big anatomy exam, she and I sat stuffing our brains in the otherwise empty anatomy classroom. Students sometimes studied there after hours, me hoping the ghosts of anatomy lessons past would fill my brain with the name of the specific protuberance of the elbow joint that served as the attachment point for the triceps muscle and other such valuable knowledge. She stood up and stretched her arms over her head, comfortable in her sweatpants, sweatshirt and sneakers.

"Boy, I wish I could trade places with you right now, Char . . . you don't seem stressed at all! Look, you're still cheery. You must have studied all weekend—are you ready?" I was like a coiled spring, feeling woefully underprepared despite my exhausting hours of effort. My jeans pinched my waistband, the payoff of my junky eating habits lately. A stiff tag at the back of my neck from my blouse was bugging me. I kept forgetting to cut that off when I was near a pair of scissors. A low-grade ache wrapped around my forehead, pulsing like an ailing neon sign.

Charmaine grinned pleasantly as she related how she had spent the weekend in the hospital, the result of an intestinal bleed. As matter-of-fact as if describing the contents of her backpack, she explained that she was a hemophiliac, an inherited factor VIII deficiency, which had allowed Friday night's enchilada and spicy nacho dinner to become a life-threatening event. Her inability to properly clot her blood required an ER trip for a blood transfusion with its precious clotting factors whenever she bled anywhere. She'd had a number of transfusions since she was young, sometimes twice a week for weeks at a time when she'd get a wrist or elbow bleed, she said.

She laughed at my astonishment. Her fine, sandy hair fell around her child-like, oval face. Her gentle expression flattered her soft features. She assured me she was fine with her condition and that's just how it was for her. She wasn't careless but she refused to place limitations on her life. She wore a helmet around her horse and especially when riding. Charmaine added, almost as an afterthought, that she was a diabetic too and needed to give herself daily insulin injections. Of her four brothers and three sisters, two others were hemophiliacs, one was a diabetic and she was the only one with both conditions. "I hit the jackpot!" she teased.

I was struck as if by gale-force winds. My eyes didn't leave her face. At that moment she was so natural, so unembellished. "Char, I didn't know. How does your family handle this? How do you?"

She straightened the stack of papers balancing on the edge of her desk. "We're really just a pretty average bunch. Things are fairly routine these days—we know the ropes. We've all been able to adapt the family schedules around events and doctor appointments that sometimes come up. God has blessed us richly with our incredible family. My dad is a teacher. And now, my mom's actually studying to become a minister, so we're both involved in our schooling at the same time!"

I knew Charmaine's Christian faith to be much more animated than mine. Hers was clearly a life reflecting her spiritual beliefs. In her was housed a quiet, fierce trust in God for all things in her life. Never one to utter an unkind thought, she was a soothing presence with just a few words to those around her. Now I understood where that came from.

We were quiet for a minute. I looked down at my hands, where I slid my favorite sterling patterned ring back and forth over one of my swollen knuckles. The radiator must have been overheating again in the classroom.

"Don't worry, Monica, I'm fine. And I'll never be separate from the animals. It's a need, like food and water for me." She leaned her arms far forward to stretch her back. "Guess we should get back to business. Here, let's go over the innervations and venous supply to the lower hind limb of the dog."


It did not turn out to be an easy exam and much of the class had difficulty. Neither of us felt good afterward nor did either of us achieve high scores. We commiserated and vowed to somehow improve our study methods. Frustrated, we knew that we'd need to bring our grades up. We had all been told during orientation that one D on one test could get a student kicked out of vet school and neither of us was left with a huge buffer after that test. For me, it was a rude awakening that I was no longer at the top academically, that A's no longer even seemed within my reach, that I was surrounded by the intense brainpower of my very talented classmates and colleagues at Cornell. I kept looking down for my safety net, but this was the real deal. In my ever-since-childhood dreams of caring for puppies and kittens and healing sick animals, I didn't plan on the emotional wallop to my sense of self.

As overwhelming as the academic stress could be, veterinary school did offer fun distractions, vital to balance our spirits. Hidden acting skills of many a vet student were tapped for the traditional class skits, performed several times a year to lampoon key professors on their birthdays. Our scriptwriters Cindy, Marcia, Maryanne and Mary combined wits to turn quirks of our professors' behavior into chunks of gold. The zany scenarios incorporated musical themes and actors always sported embarrassing costumes. One show, themed around the Muppet Babies for our Muppet-loving embryology professor Dr. Noden, required a group of tall, handsome classmates to wear improvised diapers over their shorts. Charmaine and I joined the sizable group of entertainers in our class. The howls of laughter made us feel human again for a while.

Friday or Saturday nights might be flavored by house parties at one of the two vet student fraternities, which Char and I would attend, with guests dancing, relaxing or laughing. There was the time Tim and Bernie passed out a couple of plates and plastic forks at the party, saying there was chocolate cake in the kitchen. Word spread and a line soon formed for the nonexistent dessert, those two guys off in the corner, snickering. Char was a jovial participator, even a willing prankster herself on the weekends she stayed on campus. Other times she went back home two hours away to visit her family and pets.

Charmaine owned a horse that she kept in a barn a couple miles from the college. She loved her above almost all else. Occasionally I joined her for the feeding chores. The first time I came along, we rode together in her timeworn, pale green Oldsmobile.

"How can you afford to keep a horse?" I asked her. A box of tissues, her epidemiology textbook and some cracker wrappers sat between us on the bench-style front seat. As we stopped in front of the barn, I unbuckled my threadbare passenger belt. Now worried for her, I noted that her seat was thankfully outfitted with a better belt, one with a shoulder strap. Surely she should take no chances.

"Well, other than her food bills, these friends of mine—a married couple—let me keep her in their barn here free in exchange for my feeding and mucking all the horses' stalls."

When we entered, she pointed out a proud chestnut mare prancing in the nearby field with four other horses.

"That's Dancer over by the fence. Isn't she gorgeous?" Char stood, proudly gazing at her.

"Look how she dances when she sees you! She's so tall and beautiful, Char."

"Except for the mud where she rolls, but that's a losing battle some weeks." She handed me a pitchfork.

Together we made quick work of cleaning out the stalls and then added fresh bedding and hay to eat. The horses came running when she whistled for them. She led each to its own stall, sang a separate one-verse song to each, scratched their foreheads and locked them all down for the afternoon. She explained how she had made up a different song for each horse, which she sang every night to them—it made them feel more loved, she said.

The stunning vista up on a hill featured the horse paddocks and more gently sloping hills beyond. The air was brisk enough for me to feel uncomfortable and winter hadn't even hit Ithaca yet. I could only imagine her up here twice a day in this "lake effect" region of upper New York State.

"Char, how are you gonna like this when it's snowing out and freezing?"

"No problem," she smiled, pulling up on the zipper of her barn coat. "This is my third year with this arrangement since my last year undergrad and my year between, working. It clears my mind and I feel so connected with these guys." She shut off the last of the light switches.

"Before we leave, Monica, there's one more animal you have to see."

She moved through a side door to a smaller room in the barn. "This is Ringo."

"What a huge sheep!"

"Yeah, he's a breeding ram. Pretty good genetic lines. Don't come too close until he knows you. He and I are good buddies, but you have to watch these intact males."

"Just like their human counterparts, right?" We giggled.


Later in the school year, spring thankfully hinted its arrival. People had told me that with a good wool sweater and a little time, winter would thicken my blood, but only the thin version continued coursing through my veins.

"Let's go take a break for a bit," I whispered to Charmaine, she being seated next to me at one of the long library tables.

Primed for a well-deserved interlude from the afternoon study routine, she agreed. "Wanna get some air?"

"Sure." I had intended to simply walk the halls leading to the vending machines, one that sold disgusting-but-caffeine-bearing coffee and another, those synthetic orange cracker packets. However, it might sharpen the mind to get a nice chill instead.

"Glad there aren't any exams for the next two weeks. Maybe I'll get to pick up my guitar." I said. I shoved my hands in my coat pockets as we left the building. The many paths around the vet school and lower campus offered a choice of level or hilly, all scenic distractions from the study tables. Today we chose level. I had trouble getting the simple bumper sticker line, "Ithaca is Gorges," out of my mind whenever I jogged or walked around. The terrain varied but never disappointed. Rumor had it that undergrads couldn't help but earn well-developed calf muscles and decent cardiovascular fitness just in the course of changing classes on the hilly lower campus.

"I agree. I should have you get me started on guitar. I'm gonna learn to play one of these days!" She bent to tie her wayward shoelace. "Hey, how's everything going with you? Are things well with you and your boyfriend?"

"I don't know, Char. I really care for him a lot but I just don't know if I'm happy."

"Tell me . . ." Her voice was sympathetic.

"I guess . . .well . . . I'm not really sure I trust him. When we first started seeing each other, we were both dating someone else. I broke up with the guy in Virginia I'd been seeing undergrad, even though he and I had said we'd date other people. I couldn't deal with the emotions of two relationships. Supposedly Pete broke up with his long-distance girlfriend at the same time. But I'm not sure I believe him."

"There has to be a reason you feel that way, though?" She quickened our pace.

"It's odd. His roommates have tried to hint to me and told me to be careful. And like last weekend he was evasive and unavailable the entire weekend and it really made me wonder if she was visiting him or something. But then I listen to what Pete tells me that it's only me that's important to him and I believe him."

I looked down at the salt-stained pavement, wondering if I could extract from her the answers I was struggling for, even what I couldn't verbalize.

She touched my shoulder. "This is hard. I know he's a good guy and funny and handsome. And you care for each other."

We turned back for the college.

"You know what else I feel guilty about, Char? I have a secret crush on someone else . . . " I admitted sheepishly.

"Who?"

"Of course I'd never do anything about it. But am I horrible or what? Does everyone have little crushes at some point even when they're seeing someone else? Is it a matter of what you do about it?"

"Of course! You don't live in a bubble, you know. Maybe you're not satisfied in that relationship. You're a beautiful person, inside and out, and I don't think you should cut yourself off. Now *who*?" she persisted.

"Oh, you know Keith in our class." The first time I had met him had been at a rocky swimming quarry hangout in one of the gorges prior to the start of classes. We were all in swimsuits and I couldn't help but notice his muscled pecs and biceps from throwing lobster pots on New Hampshire's seacoast all summer. The bright sun had illuminated his dark eyes and my initial impression had been what an intriguing person he seemed. "We're really good friends. There's a lot more to him than what's on the surface. Kinda like, if there was someone in trouble, he'd be there in a heartbeat and know exactly what to do and at the same time make it all seem like it was no big deal."

Keith was brilliant. He sat in the back of the classroom, appearing detached, yet indeed concentrating deeply on each lecture. He frequently drew quick sketches in the margins of his notes to improve his comprehension, each a masterpiece. Usually silent in class, once every several months Keith would interject an astute analysis to the class discussion, leap years ahead of most of us. While Charmaine sat mostly in the front, I often sat near Keith, liking the more relaxed back-of-the-classroom atmosphere. It calmed me. It was a comradely bunch in the rear rows that often studied at the long tables together in the library, Keith and I among them, sharing notes and melting into fits of laughter at the antics of some.

Two class favorites were Mark and Jack, who authored a running daily line of hysterical insults to one another, always ending with "You shut up," "No, *you* shut up." Their endearing words for one another included "fathead" and "you are SO ugly," "no, *you're* ugly." They sat next to each other in nearly every lecture. At first I wondered what was real and what was gag and then I understood and they made me laugh the hardest anyone had made me laugh, ever. The bits were all toned in humor so dry and wit so sharp, the cast of Monty Python would be proud. It was all in the delivery of the lines. I appreciated the intelligence that went into the timing, the wording and the underlying innuendos. Once, in the necropsy room, someone had doctored that room's copy of our class roster photo so that over Mark's name was a photo of a gorilla. We all suspected Jack. Mark loved it.

Except for Keith's delayed hearty laugh, which itself would make our class break into a second round of laughter, everything about Keith's demeanor was understated—quiet, kind and sincere, with a wicked sense of humor. After yet another difficult anatomy exam, I had asked him if I could use his test paper to learn from my mistakes. He agreed, but only if I swore not to tell anyone his score—a near-perfect 98. That was tantamount to a near-perfect SAT score or a near-perfect lunar landing. He began tutoring me each week in large-animal anatomy and I really hoped this would help me.

"Keith is a great guy," she said, "Do you think he likes you that way?"

"We're good friends but he's dating someone else now in a different department on campus. She seems really sweet." I thought of the mixer many of us from our class had attended where Keith had brought her and I had tried to make her feel welcome.

"Thanks for hearing me out, Char." I yanked hard at a strand of my hair stuck in the clasp of my necklace, frustrated with it. We were back inside the lobby of the school now. It had been an invigorating walk. I felt lighter, though no closer to resolution about my love life.

"Do you want to come to the barn with me in another hour or so?" Charmaine asked as we settled back in front of our books, our cheeks rosy.

"Thanks, but I think I'll stay here and get some more work done." I was still scared I would fail. How I wished for my own Great Gazoo on my shoulder telling me exactly how to spend each hour of the day and how to resolve my personal relationships. And how I longed for the academic success I had previously known.


Over summer break, Charmaine and I exchanged letters. She was thrilled to be putting in long hours working with Dr. Freeman whose mixed-animal veterinary practice was, incredibly, next door to her family's home. He had promised her a job as soon as she graduated. She boarded Dancer at a neighbor's barn just three houses down from her during the summer. It was perfect. She sent me an exquisite gold-laid leaf necklace she had just bought at a county fair. It was a cottonwood leaf perfectly preserved, all the leaf's veins intact and somehow covered in the metal. This was my favorite piece of jewelry all summer. As it hung on my shirtfront, the necklace was a quiet token to me of the tiniest seed that grows into the biggest of trees. I sent her the sterling ring I loved.

School's return came quickly. While I had enjoyed my summer's three simultaneous veterinary-assistant jobs, it was exciting to start in school again and good to see my friends. I missed her.

Charmaine and I lunched together the first free Saturday at our favorite little pub.

"You look great! How the heck are you?" I asked. How good to finally get caught up with her. Her fair skin glowed with a tan and her sun-streaked hair was longer than I'd seen it before. "How's the house you're staying in?"

"Oh, it's great. You should come over," she answered.

Our chili arrived hot.

She blew on her spoonful and asked about my family. She told me about hers and how fast the summer had gone. She'd had so many great animal experiences.

We talked about Pete and how evasive he was that summer and that he and I never even visited one another. His brother didn't know who I was when I called his house. It felt fishy. I told her I might have some hard choices to make in that department but I wasn't sure what was right. I didn't look up, feeling ashamed.

She tilted her head thoughtfully. "Monica, I wish you were happy. I wish you could enjoy yourself. Is it possible that you and he have different agendas? Different outlooks on what your relationship means?"

I felt tears rising. I knew what she was trying to make me see and she was being so gentle about it. I finished my last two oyster crackers. Why was this so hard for me? It sure didn't feel right, no question. I looked up and tried to change the subject. "Okay, woman, and what about you? Any leads in the love life department?"

"No, but I don't have to right now. I'm quite happy—between the animals and what I'm learning in class, it's what I've always dreamed of doing. And uncomplicated!"

Char's clearheaded goal was the true pursuit of knowledge. She laughed and protested when I compared the two of us to Confucius, the wise sage, and one of his eager but foolish disciples, with all my fretting and obsessing over my grades and the men in my life. It was good we'd had the time to talk. We paid our tab, hugged and went our ways.


Three weeks later, I grabbed her arm when I saw her in anatomy class Monday morning. "I've got to talk to you, Char."

We had minutes before the start of class.

"What's up?" She pushed her pack under her seat and joined me.

We walked out into the hall and around the corner, where I explained. I had decided to break up with Pete after reading a note on his dresser that made it clear there was someone else in his life. It was the kick in the pants I needed. I would do it that day and let her know. I wanted a pep talk from her.

"Are you okay?"

"Yeah, a little queasy but once it's done, I'll move on. It's just gonna be getting the words out. He's a nice guy and I still care for him but this is what I know is right. We should get back to class but I'll tell you what happens. Hey . . . and thanks for helping me through this. I couldn't do it without you."

"I'm really proud of you," she said.

Later, I called Charmaine from my house. "I did it, Char. He seemed surprised. I didn't tell him about the letter but said I felt like he wasn't being straight with me. It wasn't that hard. Anyhow, I feel pretty depressed. Not like I want him back. Just like I couldn't see it for what it was or didn't want to believe it." I fought my tears as I twirled the phone cord with my fingers. "You could see how foolish I was all along, couldn't you?"

"No, not at all! Use this experience to learn, that's all. You don't have anything to be ashamed of. You're a trusting person and that's a beautiful thing. You had to do this one on your own and you did." Her voice smiled, "Do you still have an eye out on your other crush, hint, hint?"

"Well . . . " I countered, "Keith and his girlfriend broke up this summer. He and I are such good friends and it's not all the superficial stuff. I wouldn't mind at all going out with him. Just maybe not right away."

"That's a start."

She decided that I would just have to make him dinner, despite my protests that I couldn't cook well enough. With some prodding, we uncovered that I made a decent lasagna and that was to be my future weapon of choice.

I followed Charmaine's advice and eventually found a natural opportunity in the next couple months to cook lasagna at Keith's place. And, thanks to Charmaine's push, that was the start of our long courtship built on the base of mutual respect and strong friendship.

🐾 🐾

The first day back from Christmas break, our classmate Luba stood up to make an announcement before a lecture.

"You guys, Charmaine's in the hospital in Rochester."

I paled. Luba, normally laid-back and gregarious, was stern and serious.

"She was kicked by a ram and shattered her tibia a week ago. She needed her leg surgically reconstructed. Unfortunately, she's developed some serious intestinal problems—they think she might have picked up a hospital infection. Maybe we could send her a care package and everyone sign this card I'll send around."

God.

It had been a whirlwind Christmas break at home, with a big family trip to Disney and I hadn't written or phoned Charmaine. Charmaine was going to spend most of her break in Ithaca and take care of the animals. She had said how much she enjoyed being on campus when all was quiet and no studies so she could enjoy the surroundings and spend more time with Dancer. I knew Luba was quite friendly with Charmaine too and her family lived near Char's. I could barely wait for the end of class so I could pump Luba for information. She knew nothing else.

That evening I called the Moshers' home to pass on my best wishes for a speedy recovery. Mr. Mosher promised to tell Charmaine that I called but wasn't sure if she was up to taking phone calls yet. Two hours later, my phone rang. It was her.

"Hey, there," she said, subdued.

"Charmaine! What happened to you? I just found out!"

"It hasn't been an easy week."

"Well, I'd say! You poor thing. You must be in so much pain! And what's going on with your intestines?" I pictured her in the stereotypical cast and traction seen in television dramas.

"They said I should be back home in a few days on antibiotics. I'm just pretty nauseous. The leg hurts."

"Was it Ringo? You tell me which ram did this to you, and I'll make him wish he'd never so much as looked at you cross-eyed!"

She laughed gently, "Yes it was. I don't know what spooked him. I wasn't looking up. Next thing I knew, he got me."

"What did you do, Char?! How'd you get help?"

"Well, I heard it crack and knew it was broken, and there was no one around, so I dragged myself into my car and drove to Tompkins County Hospital. When I got there, I just blew my horn until someone came and got me."

"Aaaaaargh!!! Ouch! That's on the other side of Ithaca and around the lake!" I was queasy imagining her efforts.

"You do what you have to. Once I was in the car, I didn't want to have to get back out or move if I was somewhere that couldn't help me right away. I knew that I'd need blood and they could do that there. At least it was my left leg, and I could kind of prop up my right elbow to balance myself a little on some books on the seat while I drove."

"Thank goodness there's no stick shift in that boat of yours." God. The agony she must have felt.

"They transferred me to Rochester before surgery. My blood sugar's been a little whacky since I'm not eating well but the doctors are on top of things." She sounded tired.

"I should let you go, Char. How can I stay in touch?" I knew she was only letting on to a portion of the pain she was feeling.

"Oh, I'll be back in a couple of weeks."

"Have your parents call if you need anything. Listen, get some sleep with healing dreams, okay? I'll see you soon. Love you, kiddo."

A couple of weeks became a couple of months. After the intestinal problem, her liver was seriously affected. Biopsies showed an infection with a fungus called histoplasma. It had invaded several body organs. Because systemic histoplasmosis will spread, damaging the lungs and nervous system, treatment with an antifungal agent, amphotericin B, was necessary. This was not easy—an intravenous infusion six hours a day, three days a week, for nine months. Doctors speculated that she silently harbored the fungus since a trip she took to Brazil several years earlier. The infection had become activated due to the stress of her severe injury.

Our class sent several care packages—photos of events, cheery cards. We were informed whenever Charmaine's progress changed. I contacted the family every few weeks and Char wrote occasionally. Sometimes she felt up to phone calls and at times asked me to find out medical information for her from the vet school library, which referenced many human medical texts as well as veterinary. What did these liver test results mean? Could the amphotericin cause her electrolyte pattern on her blood work to remain abnormal? I would make it my mission to find out as much as I could for her whenever she asked. The plan was for Char to take a leave of absence from school for a year and a spot would remain open for her to pick up where she left off. I missed her tremendously.

In April, Luba announced to the class that there was now involvement with Charmaine's heart. A nurse had accidentally bolused a rapid dose of a heart medication that was supposed to be given slowly over fifteen minutes. This had caused Charmaine to bolt up in bed and lapse into a coma. She was in the intensive care unit, prognosis unknown. I sat in the back of the classroom, tears dotting my notes. I didn't take in a word of that lecture.

Thankfully, she regained consciousness within a week, the worst danger past, but her body was severely weakened. All for me to do was send her letters when I could. I knew she would enjoy them even though she couldn't respond.

It was the start of our junior year when I next saw Charmaine in the student parking lot. She and the person with her were almost upon me before I recognized her. She looked frail and thin and walked slowly with a cane. Her hair rested in a loose ponytail, her skin tone pale. Ecstatic, I held her in a tight hug.

"Charmaine! What a surprise! How the heck are you?!? Are you back for good?"

"No," she laughed quietly. "I'm okay. It's been a long haul, I'm staying with Linda overnight. I wanted to come by and visit a few friends and see Dancer now that I'm feeling stronger. I wanted to surprise you. I was gonna call you later."

"Can I take you to lunch or dinner?"

"No, but why don't you come to Linda's house tonight. I'd like to talk to you."

"I'll be there."

I watched her and Linda walk away. Char moved slowly and deliberately.

That evening I sat spellbound on Linda's couch touching Char's sleeve while she detailed her coma's ordeal.

"You may not really understand this . . . during the time I was unconscious, I was actually battling Satan. It was terrifying. He was trying to get me to say that certain Bible passages were lies and that love wasn't real. Like Corinthians 'Love is patient and kind; it is not jealous or proud. Love is not happy with evil, but is happy with the truth.' And from John, 'Let us love one another, because love comes from God. Whoever loves is a child of God and knows God. Whoever does not love does not know God, for God is love.' Day and night I battled him as he tried tactic after tactic to get me to deny these truths and others. I held firm."

An eerie clamminess made the back of my neck tingle. This was intensely personal and horrifying.

"When he finally realized that I was out of reach, he told me he would go after my family next if I didn't give in to his lies and say the things he wanted. He had found my Achilles heel but I knew I couldn't budge. Somehow love transcended all and he finally left me. That's when I fully woke up."

"Oh, Charmaine!"

"My father told me that as the coma was easing, he put a large metal cross into my hand, hoping it might help me, having no idea what I was going through. He said I fingered it all over and flung it across the room like a knife. What *I* remember is Satan handing me a perverted crucifix which I disposed of because of how hideous it was. It was a short time after then that I came back. I was drained afterward and mostly slept for a couple of days."

She sat on her friend's couch, leaning toward me. I sat, fixated on her thin face, entranced.

"Oh, this was so much worse for you than I knew! Do you believe this to be a truly supernatural encounter or do you think it could be like a dream, something the mind can experience in a coma?" I asked gently. As deep as her spiritual faith was, she was also a woman of science, not taken by fantasy.

"All I know is what I went through, Monica. It was absolutely real to me. I know it was not a dream. I was told at the hospital that people really have no memory of their unconscious time but I remember this."

"I don't know how you endured so much. It's so unfair for all this to happen to you!" My cheeks prickled.

Her conviction was firm, "I'm in God's company. He'll never leave me or my family. Or you too for that matter."

Then no words.

I didn't want to leave but she was fatigued. Her face was drawn.

"Are you doing all right? How's school for you?" she asked as I got up to go.

"Yeah, school's going much better and Keith's great. I got a high A on my recent pharmacology exam—can you even believe it? Keith's steady, steady, steady technique of truly focusing and learning each day's lessons as they are taught has really helped me. I'm more present and review right away. Less cramming facts and more understanding concepts. I wish you were there with me at that favorite table of ours in the library." I clasped her hand into my two as she stood. "Charmaine, I feel like I should somehow be doing more for you but I don't know what. I miss you so much."

"You've done more than enough. The letters and the packages mean a ton to me. My parents think you're great."

"I never know if I'm a bother when I call the house—"

"Never."

I held her close to say good-bye and kissed her forehead. "You're gonna keep getting stronger, Char, I know it. You have a lot waiting here for you to come back to, and everybody's sending you strength. We'll study together." Then I left.

Mr. Mosher telephoned me at home one evening several weeks later.

"Hi, Mr. Mosher! How's Char?"

"Well, Monica, there's a new problem. The amphotericin has sped up the retina changes that her diabetes causes. She's losing her eyesight rapidly. But the doctors think she will benefit from laser surgery. They'll do one eye at a time."

"Oh . . . will there be permanent vision loss?"

"They don't know."

How would she ever get back to school or her beloved critters, to Dancer, I thought. "How's she handling this?"

"You know, one of the main things that keeps her going is that she's gonna return one day." He sounded worried.

"Is she up for any visitors?" I'd drop everything and go there that weekend.

"I wish I could say yes, but she's so sick, I would hate for you to make the trip out here. The hospital's another hour from our house."

"I understand. I'll stay in touch. Feel free to call me anytime."

Our class was grim as I announced the news. We sent another card around. We sent some music tapes too, and I found a Bible on tape for her.

She never improved.

She called me one evening in late January.

"Hi, Monica."

"Char? I didn't recognize your voice. How are you?"

"I've got pneumonia. The doctors today drew blood to see if I have AIDS. It's gonna be three weeks until the results are back." She paused, caught up in a coughing spell. "Can you find out some information for me about AIDS and call me at my hospital room?"

"Oh, of course. I'll call you this time tomorrow. Are you having trouble breathing?" I was trying to remain composed despite the deep dread infiltrating my guts.

"No, just this cough. And my ribs ache."

"I'll find out as much as I can for you, sweetie. Don't you worry now about anything."

On a desperate mission to find answers to her questions, I spent the rest of that evening at the library, doing one of the most important literature searches of my school career. It was early 1986, and an AIDS diagnosis was in its infancy, I suppose not very high on doctors' early list of differential diagnoses for Charmaine. I knew some about HIV through my coursework and its comparison to animal immunosuppressive diseases. The more detailed information I was finding out through my search was definitely not good. I read through every reference I could find, layering books and periodicals on the table, a disheveled madwoman searching for light within those familiar stacks. My grim panic rose. Her precious T cells. AIDS fit so many of her health problems the past eighteen months—the bizarre fungal infection, the liver and heart issues, her hemophilia and resultant history of blood transfusions, the inability to fight everyday infections, her frail body and now the pneumonia!

When I called her the next evening, I gently told her only bits of what I'd found, just enough to specifically answer the questions she'd asked. What cell lines were affected? What body systems? The incubation period? What drugs were being used? We'd always spoken the truth to each other. When she asked if there was a cure in sight, I told her I didn't know. She thanked me, saying this all eased her mind, just her understanding the disease more.

Two weeks later, Mr. Mosher informed me that Charmaine was quite ill. The pneumonia wasn't responding, her doctors predicting that the end was imminent. She had required one CPR resuscitation already and she decided to change her status to DNR—do not resuscitate. Her family maintained a twenty-four-hour bedside vigil. Mr. Mosher agreed that she might like a quick phone call.

I could hear each inspiration, each expiration as she struggled. I did most of the talking.

"Charmaine, you know how much I love you!" I told her, my voice hiding how my heart was breaking. How to choose what to say to her?

"Mm-hmm," she responded. Words were indecipherable.

"Char, we all miss you. You know, they're still keeping a spot open here for you."

I imagined she smiled.

"You're one of the most incredible people in my life, Char. You've helped me and taught me so much. My life is so much better because of you." I worried I was taxing her as she continued her forced respirations. "I'll let you go back to resting, sweetie. You just relax and know you are surrounded by people who love you. I'm praying so hard for you. I love you so much!"

We hung up and I ached. I stared at the phone on its hall table for a long time as the weight of those moments crushed me.

Two evenings later, Mr. Mosher called me again.

"Hi, Mr. Mosher!" I said too enthusiastically. "How are you?"

"Not too good. We lost Char this morning. Barbara and I were gathered around her, singing hymns, saying prayers, just being together."

"I'm so sorry . . ."

His voice sounded so strong, my stomach became ice.

"I'll tell my classmates and the office," I somehow spoke.

"That would help. The funeral will be on Thursday and anyone from the school is invited. We'll be having a reception at our house afterward, which Char wanted."

I wrote down directions and hung up shattered. With my back against the wall, I slid to the floor and held my hands over my face. Quiet tears trickled around my fingers. I supposed prayer would be proper then, but it seemed hollow. Keith came, and we were wordless together, that day in February.

The following day, I announced the news to the class, which was met by stunned silence and several bowed heads. Our instructor for that session had difficulty beginning his lecture.

A handful of us students and teachers carpooled the two hours to the funeral in the cold rain. Fingering the gold-leaf necklace she had given me, I marveled again at how the artisan had possibly preserved the fallen leaf's each detail. The potential it represented, the beauty. The rain turned to ice, then snow as she was buried. A pebble lodged in my flat dress shoe at the cemetery but I left it in there. The services and then the reception afterward were celebrations of Charmaine's life, reinforcing the loving family life to which she had been privy. During the drive back to Ithaca, I slept.

I bumped into my classmate Claire in the hallway a few days after Charmaine's funeral.

"Hey," he said in his gentle way, "How were things at her funeral?"

Like pulled seams in a flimsy garment, I unraveled. Tears tumbled down my face as we stood outside the library.

"I'm sorry to upset you," he said, helpless, this large man kindly supporting me. He put an arm around my shoulders while I sobbed in the school hallway. He had been an unwitting catalyst to my mourning, which had thus far eluded me. To that point, I'd shed only minimal tears, surprised at my own ability to operate so smoothly.

I remained in close contact with Mr. and Mrs. Mosher after Char's funeral. I never asked the results of the HIV test, although I assumed the disease to be a given. That spring, I accepted Mrs. Mosher's invitation to join the family for Easter weekend. Several of her kids would be away at college, so there would be plenty of room at the house. She asked me to play a song at her small rural church's Easter services where she had recently become a minister. There would be a church breakfast afterward.

Mrs. Mosher showed me to Charmaine's room, where I would sleep. She bestowed upon me Char's stethoscope and the blue down vest she usually wore to the barn, both precious treasures to me. She showed me the guitar that Char had begun to play as her eyes failed her, the instrument restrung to accommodate her left-handedness. I smiled—she had said she would play guitar one of these days and she did it.

There was a photo on Char's dresser of handsome Iver, the Devil Dog, her much-loved Doberman who bonded to only her. Besides constantly being at her side around her family's house, Iver had served as a guide dog of sorts for Charmaine as her eyesight dwindled. She had begun taking him to an obedience class, and he absorbed that. Every day that she wasn't in the hospital, she used her cane to visit Dancer who was for the time being housed in her neighbor's barn. Iver instinctively led her around the mud puddles to where she needed to be. A few months after the photo was taken, when Charmaine was very ill and hospitalized, Iver was hit by a car in a freak accident and killed instantly. When Mrs. Mosher had first come home from the hospital that day without Char, Iver ran around the family car looking for her. Searching for Char still, he dashed out into the street. Mrs. Mosher waited a while to tell Charmaine about it, but when she heard the news finally from her hospital bed, Char was accepting—a dream she had with screeching brakes made her mindful in advance of hearing the real truth. Iver was less than two years old when he died, a young, bright flame whose time was short but whose job was to tend to Charmaine.

In Charmaine's bed that night, I wondered if I would dream about her. I felt so close to everything she loved. It wasn't to be.

Before the crack of dawn Sunday, the Mosher family and I awoke and readied ourselves for the mountaintop sunrise service Mrs. Mosher was to lead, literally as the sun came up. At her request, I opened the service with a song of my choosing, a poignant favorite of mine from my church folk group days, a contemporary religious folk song, "Here I Am," by Tim Schoenbachler. With the first ray of light, I started the song: "Here I am, oh Lord, send me." The dozen or so participants in the service heartily joined in with the chorus.

As I sang the second verse, I noticed from the hills an electrifying echo of voice and guitar strains. The group again joined in their part as reverberations sent chills down my spine.

An ending last line of the final verse, "But have no fear for I am with you . . . in storm and gentle breeze . . . in storm and gentle breeze," had a sustained high note, the sound of which fed upon itself as I sang out with all my heart. When the song ended, the sun was fully visible over the top of the hill, and my hair was tossed by a soft, warm wind.


A tap on the office door lifted me from my reverie. It was almost time to start up with afternoon appointments. I'd go through this day more aware, richer.

I hoped I'd run into Darryl in town sometime. She would never know how timely her visit with Alex was that day. Perhaps it was just this one time that I was supposed to know her. We would have to see.

Maybe that anniversary remembrance card would still get to Char's parents on time. I'd be sure to make it to the mailbox on my way home tonight.

# SEVEN

## *WINTER*

My first six months in Norwich, I lived at the top of a large hill, around the backside of the town center and post office, six miles up Thompson Lake Road, six miles from the animal hospital. My neighbor across the street was serene Thompson Lake. The view from the non-winterized, A-frame lodge I rented stopped my breath short. The far side of the lake was backed by an untainted view of Thompson Mountain, abutted by neighboring hills. The vista remained unspoiled by development, traffic or even proper roads and I absorbed the spectacle daily.

The splendid stillness of the early morning greeted me as I stepped out into the driveway early each day for work. This was a sacred time of day. My eyes fixated on the clear water rimmed only with vegetation and trees. Morning shadows stretched like bands trying to reach the other side. Behind the lake sat voluptuous Thompson Mountain, looking like a too-perfectly painted movie background, her rounded crown and visible tree lines beckoning the day hiker to experience her trails.

Winter was the kicker. It stomped in. This season in Norwich was more extreme than any place I'd ever lived so I felt virtuous for trudging through it. Winter for me was a personal challenge since my body seemed to require more bundling than most peoples' to remain comfortable. I loathed the weight of all those layers and bulk on my arms and body, the itch and restriction. I'm sure it was a sensory issue for me in that mine were over-wired but the pervasiveness of my irritation served as my silent penance. Moosehead and Amos tried to help me stay warm by snuggling up on my bed at night. This was a winter world different than any I'd experienced. Official mid-winter regional thermometer readings averaged twenty degrees Fahrenheit, not counting the harsh wind-chill factors that regularly blew through the region, and usual snowfall accumulations totaled ninety to ninety-five inches. That winter, I learned the value of long underwear, multiple layers of clothing and wool socks. The winds were brutal. With every possible body part covered, some in triplicate, and with some mental psyching, I was able to tolerate the dash down the twenty log-lined front steps out to the car to start the engine then back up to the house for a few more minutes until it was time to go. Many days seemed unbearably frigid and I wondered how it was that everyone else apparently functioned so evenly up here every day. Then we would get a break in the weather pattern, a couple of days when it was bright, sunny and fantastic, there was no wind, the air smelled crisp and I'd think, "I can do this, I can live this." I tried not to let it show but my cold intolerance shaded every pleasure for me and it was my personal challenge, my onus to learn to live in harmony with this region. The admission price to all this magnificence.

In winter, the lake transformed itself. Ice crystals tinkled on the frozen lake as I stood for a moment listening on the road's edge in the early morning before opening my car door or making any noise. Those delicate notes, like miniature glasses breaking, could be heard only if there was no breeze and one remained completely still. It was like a secret orchestra by a covert society of tiny ice musicians and my ears were witness to the show.

When frozen, the lake lent her solid back for recreational purposes. Usually a trusty four inches thick by January, snowmobilers, cross-country skiers and ice fishermen found her a sturdy base. I took the new cross-country skis that Keith had given me with the hope that I could find a sport that would endear me to this season. Alone, resembling a wobbly newborn deer, I learned to steady myself without the intimidation of onlookers in an overcrowded park somewhere. Sunday afternoons were best for me to practice, sometimes under sunny skies, sometimes in the company of soft flurries but mostly in complete solitude. Soon, I was gliding the flat surface comfortably, usually a peaceful half-hour at a time. A couple times, when Keith and I enjoyed the same weekend off, we traveled north up the mountain chain to one of the big ski areas, where there were miles of well-worn cross-country trails to enjoy, complete with other skiers, and I swallowed my newness and tried to blend in. Some winter afternoons remained mild, which contributed to my good cheer even as I fell, my fingers protected from the snow landing with my thick ski gloves Keith's brother Ian had given me that Christmas. We enjoyed the fitness experience and we treasured the exquisite, surround-sound beauty, mountain peaks whichever way we turned.

Then there were those people I watched in awe. Beth's husband worked for the power company and regularly climbed telephone poles when there were outages in the iciest of storms and the most whipping of winds. His job had to be done and he told me he loved being able to help so many people the way he did. The lure of ice fishing, however, for pure recreational purposes remained a mystery, an odd fascination for me. Indeed, the setting couldn't be topped, but the idea of choosing to spend a day sitting still on top of a frozen lake boggled my mind. Granted, I never tried it but then again, I probably never would. Surely one's basic metabolic rate needed to be different than what I was given. An ice thickness of at least four inches was required of the lake, usually there by late January. To fish, these individuals (almost exclusively men, from my observations) first drilled a fishing hole a few feet in diameter into the ice. Then a small wooden shack that looked like an outhouse was transported by pickup truck and placed over the hole. Some shacks housed benches, carefully placed butane heaters or lanterns, magazines, food and plenty of beer. Many fishermen teamed up in pairs or groups, a time of great camaraderie. Others found this their private respite, not to be disturbed. The lake remained peppered with several of these tiny shelters through the coldest months and conversely, their removal signaled the earliest of spring's harbingers. They became like studs on the lake, piercings to liven up her winter wardrobe. I wondered—how could these fishermen trust that the ice would hold all that weight and how did they know for sure when they must remove the shanties before the ice became too weak? Perhaps my subconscious mind was telling me that I dwelled on ice fishing a little too seriously when I had a nightmare that I was abducted and forced to sit in one of these huts, naked. I awoke with no covers on, shivering.

Snow was a constant that season. From practically the first snowfall in late November, there was a continual ground and road cover. Plows were now attached to the front grills of many of the pickup trucks the townspeople drove. The "wow" factor of any one large snowstorm was minimized by the frequency of multiple snow events. By January, I took the storms as a given, like doing the laundry, just another duty to deal with, part of the décor. Amazingly, I never missed work because of the snow and never got stranded at work, despite my unease with driving through the elements. The worst storm I experienced was when I ran out of cat food one Sunday and needed to travel from my house to the lakeside bait shop, which fortunately carried a few cans of wet food and sundry odds and ends. I'd been in once before on my way home from work one evening and bought some milk. The small, disheveled shop seemed to be open most of the time when I drove by, as far as I could tell by its lights or a car in front, even on Sundays, and in warmer weather, the owner often sat with some cronies in old chairs by the front entrance. Perhaps the man even lived in part of the building. I hoped fervently that he would be there that day despite the vicious storm. Poor Amos and Moosehead didn't have anything catlike to eat other than some milk in a dish and there wasn't anything I could cook up for them. The cupboards were pretty empty of any tasty cat morsels, not even a forgotten can of sardines to be found. My darned schedule kept me so focused on work that I hadn't made the trip into Plymouth to stock up on groceries that week, nor did I remember when I had driven home from work the night before. I really had to take the chance today that the shop would be open. The distance to the bait shop was only a flat half-mile and with the howling, bitter wind, I thought it best to drive there. In the near whiteout conditions, I concentrated as hard as I could on what I knew to be the road, though not sure which side of the asphalt my car was occupying. There were no other tracks. I wondered what the heck I was doing out there as I gripped the steering wheel hard, nerved up, but then saw the cats' faces in my mind's eye, poor things, and imagined them rubbing my legs expectantly. When I arrived and parked, the front door window looked dim but as I pushed, it opened into the dank room and the bell on it rang. My eye caught the shelf with the canned goods, and like a ray from the heavens above, the single hanging light bulb illuminated the two available flavors, super supper beef and minced turkey, the manna I had come in search of. For what seemed like several moments, I wondered what I should do if no one came into the silent room, if the door had been left inadvertently unlocked and the shop was actually closed. Should I take the cans and leave cash on the counter? A note? With his pen and his paper if I could find them? What if someone thought I was breaking in? The owner rounded the back corner of his store—his bedraggled hair and beard on a tall, thin body that smelled of cigarettes and alcohol now a heavenly image. The man barely spoke a word and never asked what brought me out in this storm for just those last four cans in his stock, but I supposed he didn't need to. Someone who carried cans of cat food in his remote bait shop for times like these had good in his soul, though I was glad to get what I needed, thank him and just leave. I wasn't sure if the store was really open or not. The total road trip took me over thirty minutes. Driving back, I intently watched the road still but with my purpose accomplished. I thought of my hungry kitties trotting over as the can opener hummed their favorite tune. It was that day that snow driving became slightly less intense for me, having conquered that trip out, the only driver on that small patch of road, able to keep my bearings. For the rest of my time in Norwich, having completed my voyage of necessity, I became a little more comfortable, figuring that in the future I could just think of the longer drives in snowstorms as a series of continuous little half-mile chunks like the one I conquered in the blizzard. I could do it that way, one little section at a time. I also planned out my cat food rations much better after that.

Amazingly, my eight-year-old Plymouth Horizon with ninety-five thousand miles on it started every morning. The heater in the car didn't work (although the defroster could eventually be coaxed into doing its job after about five miles of driving, five-sixths of my way to the animal hospital), so I kept the wool blanket that Keith's mom had given me on my lap and an ice scraper in my hand to clear the inner windshield while driving. I proceeded cautiously down the grade, especially during snows and I usually met no opposing traffic the entire way down. After a series of small repairs, my car needed a huge engine overhaul. Normally, the town mechanic, Joe Gould, came to the veterinary practice when his services were needed and lately my car was his star pupil. He would leave his car in our lot and drive the two miles back to his shop in the car he was to fix. Before the end of the day, he returned the repaired car with his reasonable charges and prognosis for future breakdowns. Nick had used Joe for years and trusted him and the convenience couldn't be beat. This repair, however, was no minor oil change and would cost way more than the car was worth, so I knew I needed to buy another car, despite my tight financial picture. Fortunately my father loaned me some money to make my down payment and I took out a car loan for the rest. It was better, my dad told me, to own a reliable new car and budget a certain amount per month than be stranded alone somewhere at the worst time possible in any type of weather. I sold the car to Joe for two hundred dollars and he was able to fix it up enough for his son to tool around town in. After that tough winter in Norwich, I thought my new Honda Civic heater was delicious when it satisfied my request for heat every single time I asked. I blasted it on to maximum, just because I could.

The single-lane road that led from my Thompson Lake home to work ran along a lovely stream part of the way. The houses on this passageway were different than the classic New England homes in town. Living conditions ranged from trailers to small shacks. As I daily passed one tiny, weather worn house, I started to notice at least four children who lived there. Their clothes hung to dry on clotheslines even in winter and the kids often played outdoors, underdressed for the weather. I wondered if there was anything I could do to help them and how. I thought about leaving a small bag of groceries now and again at their doorstep, yet I never did. I thought about stopping by and introducing myself, but it never seemed a good time for me to do so. What would I say to them anyhow? Hi, you look like you're having a tough time making ends meet. Is there some way I can help you? They'd look at me like I was from outer space, or worse, wonder who that self-righteous person was. I intended to ask Nick if he knew who they were but I always forgot when I got to work. Each time I drove by formulating what sort of charitable something I could do, I became like a plan with no action, for which I felt ashamed.

The house I lived in was originally intended for use as a lodge of sorts. There were four basic, raw bedrooms, each with two bunk beds meant for skiers, hunters or summer campers. It was barely winterized, breezy with high ceilings, however, the view out the window was stunning and food for the soul, which balanced the negatives. I shared the rent with a young businesswoman who worked about ten miles away. While she was excited for the business opportunity, she was vexed with stressful problems beyond any human's control, such as flood damage to her building once in the middle of the night. Other consuming worries for her were keeping good employees, protecting from break-ins, her driving in most every day at five a.m. and maintaining decent cash flow. I was away a lot, as was she. There were some good times together, like the time we spent a Sunday duct-taping plastic sheeting around all the windows and sliding doors at her suggestion in an attempt to lessen the heat loss and therefore our energy bills in our home. But we tended to see issues from different sides of the glass and for reasons that can probably be chalked up to personality differences, I brought out the abrasive in her, so I mostly stayed in my room to lessen the discomfort. I'm sure I drove her crazy with my disorganized paper stacks, my veterinary journals I rarely finished, the bits and pieces of things I intended to do but never had time for and my late-night comings and goings for work that must have woken her. I waited to play my guitar for the times when she wasn't there, but that restricted my favorite outlet. She was an active and intelligent Mensa member and her Mensa boyfriend seemed equally annoyed with me when he came to visit her for the weekend. After a while, I tried to plan for us to rarely run into each other, which is, sadly, how our relationship remained when she was asked whether or not she wished to renew the lease. I started a search for a new rental. Surely, we were both victims of high job stress and hopefully a different time and place in our lives would have found us able to maintain a cordial relationship. I learned that not every person can live with every other person and they can both still be good people inside.

It was almost spring and I found I needed to learn about two regional phenomena that were part of the locals' dealings. Driving in to work one morning, I noticed on the roadside a new, large orange temporary road sign bearing the words "Frost Heaves." Imagining perverse notions of frozen vomitus, I made a mental note to ask Beth that day what those road signs meant. As quickly as I hatched that thought, I bit into my tongue when my car suddenly rattled over a large, unseen mound in the road. A loud "ka-chunk" noise made me wonder whether Joe Gould would have some undercarriage work to do that day. I had discovered a frost heave the hard way. What began one day as a small hiccup in the pavement in the winter quickly evolved into the equivalent of a massive speed bump when water crept under the pavement and turned to ice. Many times the spring thaw simply reversed the problem, but until solidly warm temperatures came, no road crews were sent, so one quickly needed to memorize the location of these front-end re-aligners and either straddle them or drive around.

The other lingo lesson I learned was taught by one of our regular clients, Karen Davis, who came to the hospital for my last appointment one evening. We drew blood from three of her six lovely Labrador retrievers for heartworm checks. The days were light longer now and we were a bit punchy. Karen's dry sense of humor livened up my day with her charm, perfectly accented by her goofy dogs. These characters were jubilant yet obedient and it was evident that she constantly worked with them. She was a responsible dog breeder, trained them properly and took all the responsible steps toward ensuring that healthy, well-adjusted pups resulted. She relied on our medical guidance and I enjoyed learning from her.

"So you think we're actually headed for spring, Karen? How soon till you and I can be sunbathing together in our bikinis?" I teased while she held Sydney's elbow for me.

"That sun's been great today, hasn't it? I'd wait a bit before we strip down, though. We'll make a date in a few months. Can you imagine all the tongues wagging at the post office and village store if we parked a couple lounge chairs on the common midday? I bet there would be slow traffic driving by, especially by some of the gossip buddies that hold court at the store!" We both giggled and I couldn't lose that image. Town politics, personal or political, were favorite topics for a group of retirees that enjoyed their daily gabs. Both of us turned into tittering schoolgirls, then laughing at each other's laughter, finally dabbing tears from our eyes. Karen straightened, "Oh! By the way, Monica, watch out on your way home tonight for the black ice."

What was that, I quizzed her, still grinning. Wasn't ice just plain ice? To the contrary, she explained, black ice forms when a frozen night follows a warmish, sunny day like today. Water from melting snow makes an invisible, thin sheet of ice on a roadway at night. And that day's conditions were perfect. Up to that point, I'd never heard of it. As I drove home up the hill that night, my rear wheels suddenly slipped to the right. I had hit an unseen patch of black ice while rounding a sharp corner overlooking a steep drop into the frozen stream that lined the road's edge there. Thankfully, the tires quickly connected with solid pavement, leaving little room for error. I cautiously continued on, my heart racing, grateful for my lowered speed, thanks to Karen's forewarning—my guardian angel that night. I arrived home safely and more acutely aware. I called her the next day to thank her for her role.

As winter merged almost imperceptibly into spring, just when I was starting to believe there may be no more snowstorms, another local occurrence evidenced itself on the floors of the animal hospital—mud season. Mud season became official when the waiting room required mopping after every second or third client, when clots of dirt adorned the tresses of most longhaired dogs and when the retained grit between my fingers and under my nails after examining these dogs no longer bothered me. As the annual thaw of the snow cover proceeded, the roads and parking lots remained muddy and wet for weeks. Most cars earned a brownish hue. Wise Norwich residents wore a good pair of work boots outside. Mud season also signaled the official start of porcupine quill season.

# EIGHT

## *SWEET SAMMY*

"I let the porcupines out of their cages this morning to drum up some business," Nick teased me just before I took over calls for the weekend. He dared me to best his quill count from the weekend past. We saved our bowlfuls as badges of our late-night labors and numbered our weekly tallies on the bulletin board. He had been in the lead the past couple of weeks, his total at eighty-one. He had a definite advantage by a recent "two for one" deal in which both the family's dogs ran off together on one of his nights on-call.

Quill emergencies in dogs consumed a large amount of our energy during the warmer months of the year and there seemed to be a bumper crop these past couple of weeks. Porcupine quills were a perfect defense for these rotund, unglamorous pacifists. Some dogs, intrigued by the apparent ease with which they could approach and torment a porcupine, never learned that he who quills laughs last. It was not unusual to de-quill a dog several times in its life. I even once removed quills from the same dog three times in one day—a determined but unclever dog teamed with an owner with similar shortcomings.

The end of that particularly tiring Saturday, wrought with perplexing cases, brought blessed relief as I finally danced into my dream world at night where I had been hand-picked out of the audience by Bono to harmonize, pulled up onto center stage, he somehow reading my mind's deepest desire to be rockin' with his mega-band. My outfit was fitted and fantastic, my hair superb. The crowd was on their feet, I was in the groove and only perfect notes rang out. Bono was *holding my hand.* The telephone wakened me, initially a guitar's sound-effect for the song Bono and I were performing, then the tone becoming a cruel reality.

"Hullo?" I managed, still part of the music that was in my head.

"Is this the doctor?" the man's too-awake voice asked.

"Uh-huh." I realized now I was on my futon bed holding the telephone, not a microphone, in my hand.

"Hi . . . I'm really, really sorry to bother you at this time of night, doctor. This is Joe Stewart. My chocolate Lab, Sammy, just came back home covered in quills. I would have waited until morning to call, but he's pawing at his face, and they're everywhere on his body."

My thoughts screamed, "Well, what the *hell* were you doing awake at one-thirty in the morning to *know* he's covered with quills," but my words were a breathy, "Okay. I'll be in shortly."

Stumbling out of my fog, I griped aloud to Moosehead as I slipped on my jeans and loafers, grabbed my thick college sweatshirt from the dresser top, causing the folded-but-not-put-away laundry pile to topple and pulled on my jacket. My stupid jacket felt too snug on my arms over my stupid bulky sleeves. I should've had some clothes laid out on the floor the way firefighters do. One would think I'd have learned by now. This was my third on-call night in four days. The other two times I had late evening calls that kept me there till bedtime, but no middle-of-the-nighters until now. I hadn't even read the newspaper in days. I was at my whiniest. "There is no rest for the exhausted. No. Never a break. I don't even know what day it is other than a day I'm on duty." Moosie blinked his squinted eyes, his body outline resembling a cinnamon roll as he lay curled where my knee bend had been a moment before. He let escape a yawn, stretched his front paw onto a posh fold on the comforter and readjusted his chin on his front leg before he indignantly closed his eyes to sleep some more.

Through my open car windows, the nippy spring night air coaxed more of the remaining cobwebs from my grumpy head. I questioned how different I was at that moment than a driver impaired by substance abuse, but me by sleep fog. Sweet and dewy, the aroma was a cross between newly blossoming flora and invigorating pine. The profound quiet at that time of night stirred in me a novel awareness of the vastness of this space I was driving through, the immenseness of the surrounding mountains, like a premonition to the aura of some great spiritual event about to happen. Still, I struggled, deferring my amazement, wishing not to dwell in reverent wonderment, instead longing for my bedcovers.

Minutes later, I was in the clinic parking lot. Leaving my car, I mustered up a half-smile. "Hi," I greeted the dog's owner. In dismay, I noticed that I was standing in front of a man who could easily have graced the cover of "GQ" magazine—tall, strikingly handsome, nice shirt nicely fitted on nice physique. And there was me, disheveled, no makeup, scruffy old outfit, hair looking the way a rat's nest would if it too was clamped in a barrette and me not up for beaming any charming grins. I couldn't be any less cover-girl material. Well, it wasn't about "the look," I told myself. I was here to do a job. Surely, Nick and Beth would enjoy teasing me about the irony of this meeting when I told them later.

"And this must be Sammy."

"How could you tell?" he flashed a friendly smile with an easygoing charm. The only other person in the whole town who was awake and he was a comedian. Greeting me also was probably a dog, under a thick coat of quills, with a tail that somehow still flung from side to side. Like so many of the other quilled dogs, Sammy seemed fueled by his attempt to conquer the oddly shaped beast. His invigorated body happily displayed his trophies, oh so proud. Ignoring his total body immersion into quill-dom, Sammy swaggered enthusiastically to me as if I was the most important human that ever walked this patch of pavement. I first stood with my jaw dropped and my hand over my mouth. Never had I witnessed such a completely enveloped body. There was no use fighting the exclamation that next flew from my mouth, which quickly became a sympathetic groan. How on earth? I couldn't even imagine what precisely had occurred in that swamp. *Poor* boy, I cajoled Sammy, dropping to my knees to gingerly greet him. I recognized how badly I needed to be here getting him out of this mess and now my cordial spirits were back.

Inside in the light, I could only imagine that Sammy had refused to succumb to the porcupine's passive defense. Had he rolled on the poor creature or tossed it into the air? Did the porcupine lose this one time? Quills seemed to be embedded in every square inch of the skin covering this gregarious dog's sides, chest, tail and front legs. Save for his still-happy eyes, his face was unrecognizable as that of a chocolate Labrador retriever. His formerly brown facial features now looked like a dog returning from an acupuncture session run amok. I gently separated his jaws and viewed the evidence of his attempted porcupine midnight snack—a myriad of small and large quills implanted into his tongue, cheeks and soft palate. Still, he tried to nuzzle up to me, moving his tongue in a futile attempt to lick me. Sammy exuded the swampy, musky odor that was so familiar among the quilled, a by-product of the porcupine's fear and the delightfully mucky environs in which the adventure occurred.

Joe Stewart, seemingly of a mellow and unworried nature, was also profusely apologetic for the trouble Sammy's misadventure had caused. He told me how he'd picked up and placed down the phone receiver twice before actually dialing but knew he couldn't leave Sammy this way all night. He'd remembered Dr. Schatzle as a kindly man and hoped he'd understand the necessity for the late night call, not knowing he'd get me. He hoped I wasn't upset.

The corners of my lips turned up into a teasing smile. "Not to worry, Joe. Now that I'm awake, I can see where the party is. Sammy certainly takes the prize for number of quills on one dog in my experience." Silently, I figured I was a ringer for winning the week's quill contest. "Poor thing. Listen, if you can just help me get him up on the treatment table and hold a leg for me, I can get some anesthesia into him."

"Sure," he grinned, "but where do you want me to hold him without getting quilled myself?"

Well, just how would I find a vein on him, I wondered. It was time for the *please, God* entreaty that frequented my thoughts, quite often when approaching a challenging vein requiring a needle's entry. Maybe I wasn't so great at always getting them in at a scheduled time and place each day, but these little prayers rattled around in my head with great frequency most days.

I squatted beside Sammy on the now-muddy linoleum of the back treatment room and briskly plucked out a few quills from one front leg. He yelped but continued to waggle his tail rapidly, the back half of his body in sync with his tail's rhythm. "Good boy," I murmured. This charmer had easily won my heart. One look with that upturned face, were he a member of my own household, and he would have convinced me to walk him miles, throw him sticks endlessly, feed him ham sandwiches, croon sweet words to him and let him sleep with his head on my pillow.

We sat on the floor with sweet Sammy, barely restraining him, and I somehow found the vein to inject the anesthetic in that front leg first try. A few months ago, that might have been more of a struggle for me. Joe's height and muscles helped as he and I delicately lifted the stocky Lab's sleeping, eighty-pound frame onto the table, grabbing any available free patch. I collected a water bowl and a pair of dulled hemostats relegated to this task.

"Can I please help you?" Joe asked sincerely. "There are so many!"

"Well . . . sure. Here's another old hemostat you can use—you've got to grab the big quills at the base and pull quickly." I spoke rapidly, energized by the task ahead. "You can help me get started. A lot of this I'll have to do myself with a scalpel, though, with all those tiny buried ones."

I started with the mouth, while Joe worked on Sammy's backside and we quickly developed a rhythm. Pull quills and dip hemostat into water bowl. Pull and dip, pull and dip, pull and dip. It was not my intention to keep Joe there too long, but just enough to avoid my staying there all night, especially since his offer to help seemed to lessen some of his guilt. He told me how Sammy carried his leash in his mouth when he wanted to go for a walk and Joe hoped the roof of Sammy's mouth wouldn't be sore for too long. I heard stories of Sammy's romps and their huge backyard and the walks in the woods together and how Joe had adopted him several years ago from a Labrador rescue group as a two-year-old. Neither of us could understand how anyone could have ever given him up.

"My wife's gonna kill me!" he groaned as we worked.

"Why's that?" I asked.

A quiet flush brightened his features. His subtle cologne smelled good. His dog didn't.

"Well, she's out of town for the first time since we got married and told me specifically not to let Sammy out off the leash. I bartend and I just came home from work tonight, really tired. I thought he'd just do his thing in the yard and be right back. But he caught a scent and was off into the woods. He came back twenty minutes later like this. Now I'm in trouble." His dark eyes rolled upward as he shook his grimacing face.

I couldn't help but laugh. He really was a nice guy and I realized that if I had to be sharing a late night with someone, this wasn't a bad deal. Once I was fully awake, I didn't begrudge the necessity of this nighttime plucking session. In fact, it was gratifying to be able to so completely cure an animal's malady.

"So, how do you suppose you'll hide Sammy's stitches from her?" I countered.

"I'll have to think about that one."

We were quickly making headway on all those large quills. "Hey, Joe, he's actually beginning to resemble a dog again."

I could watch the remaining quills on Sammy's chest rise slowly and steadily with each anesthetized respiration. I was glad for Joe's help and good company but a lot of what was left was the more involved part.

"You go now. It really sped things up to have you here. Call me after you wake up, Joe. Hopefully, I'll wrap things up here in the next hour or so and I'll get some sleep myself."

"I really appreciate it, doc. Almost as much fun as going out dancing, huh?" His eyes sparkled as he turned to depart. "By the way, now that we've spent part of the small hours of the night together, shouldn't we be on a first name basis?"

I blushed and told him to call me Monica and that we'd each have to invite our significant others to join in our next late-night soiree. He said we should plan on it.

By myself now except for Sammy, I turned on the radio and hooted when I heard the song playing. Loudly I sang along, "Where the streets have no name, where the streets have no name . . ." My earlier dream state as a temporary rock star performing on stage was now borne out, only with an anesthetized dog as my audience and an AM/FM radio as my backing band. Life was good.

The usual quillectomy performed under anesthesia was completed in a few minutes to a half hour at the most. Sammy's took me two wee-morning hours. How troublesome the tiny quills were. I could feel them buried beneath the skin, but their removal was far from easy. Even when cutting directly over each with a scalpel blade, I'd often find several tissue planes to dissect through just to find it. In addition, any of the big quills that had broken needed digging out. Undoubtedly, there were at least a few quills I couldn't find, but they would probably migrate out a couple of days or weeks later. Sweet Sammy didn't know it, but he would be grateful when he woke.

Four large bowlfuls of quills, a couple dozen skin sutures and numerous raised scabs later, I was finished. There was no way that Nick's measly score for the week could touch mine. Bleary-eyed, I stopped counting at two hundred and fifty. I figured I would simply show him my bountiful yield in the morning. On the bulletin board, I drew the infinity sign.

I watched Sammy sleep after I had transferred him to the thick blanket in the cage I had set up. Sammy was much easier to swoop down off the table without all the quills in place and with gravity in my favor. "Oh, Sammy, you look much more comfortable now!" Hopefully his mouth would feel well soon but I had the sense that he would remain undeterred at mealtime—he was a Lab, after all. I knelt beside him with the cage front open and rested my head and arms across his wide shoulder. Maybe one day the timing would be right for me to have a dog of my own with a temperament just like his. Maybe if Keith and I got married. Maybe we wouldn't each be working so much so we could give a dog enough attention. Maybe I shouldn't stay in that position too long or I'd be waking up there in the morning. My bed at home would prove infinitely more comfortable.

Sammy never returned for the same problem while I was at the practice, but that was probably from the Stewarts' efforts, not Sammy's. I imagined them, tall master and stocky dog, handsome husband and his adorable wife, walking the fields together, using that leash as intended. My guess was that Sammy still had his own dog dreams about the strange animal he encountered that night . . . just waiting for another chance.

# NINE

## *SABER TOOTH*

The gentle lap . . . lap . . . lap . . . of Thompson Lake's unfrozen waters against the shore yielded soft consolation to my harried mind. In a couple of days I would be moving from the lake rental and I wished to drink in as much of this as possible. In those precious temperate months, I discovered the loons that came and the lake's tranquility provided me front-row seats to their mournful operas. I squatted at the edge of my driveway to watch, leaning against the back of my car. A sudden loud splash onto the lake and one or two of these sleek speckled flyers had landed, leaving a long, choppy wake behind. These loons were excellent swimmers and terrific in the air once they were above the trees, but they needed almost a quarter mile of water to land or take off and my jaw dropped when I witnessed one's attempts to become airborne, its rapidly moving feet running across the water's surface while the wings strained to lift its body. Just when it seemed the bird would never make it, the body rose, circled the lake a few times to achieve enough lift, then flew off. When I saw them other times, the loons sat on the lake and I'd taken their presence for granted the way seagulls inhabit the oceanside. It was later that I learned what a treat it was that they chose this lake as a favored ground, with only about a hundred and fifty breeding pairs in the state. I counted the heads while I watched, two or three. One would disappear for a minute while it fished in the lake. Just as instantly, the head popped back up a little further down the lake and the next one dove down. The loons bobbed on the ripples as they rested, like wooden decoys, and they called out in a song so sad and so clear that it seemed their hearts were breaking. Their echoes bounced back to me across the lake, these minor notes tugging at my core. I knew it was very important that the loons not feel threatened, so I tried to remain invisible and unheard by them, tiptoeing up the driveway steps, being careful not to crinkle my grocery bags in hand when I saw them on the lake. When their lakeside nesting sites were threatened, I had read, loons sometimes did a penguin walk on top of the water to the point of exhaustion to distract attention away from their nests. These loons I loved were poignant characters in nature's own Shakespearian drama. I would deeply miss all of this when I moved down the hill to the center of town, but it was my time to live elsewhere.

Keith's mother Alice and his brother Ian helped me move that Saturday to the house in town I would now be renting. We put Ian's roomy Pathfinder to good use as we made trips between the two places, the biggest chore that of lugging my futon. Ian, in his good-hearted way, was all too happy to take a trip up north, a region he loved exploring during ski season, and spend the day helping. Keith was working at his hospital that day, but Alice and Ian embraced me like family and helped me load boxes, piles and the cats from one place to the other, all of which we tried to do quietly out of respect for the loons. As we worked, I pondered novel ways to thank those two. Maybe a ski pass for Ian, and for Alice something with flowers or with birds, as both were passions of hers. I'd have to decide later.

A young contractor, David, was my new landlord and housemate. First introduced by David's mother Marge, a devoted, dog-loving client at the veterinary hospital, he and I became fast friends. I needed a place to stay for those second six months in Norwich, and my renting a room in the lovely, older Victorian he had renovated was good for both of us. Being closer to the office would make some difference in my attitude in the middle of the night. David's place was a mile and a half and less than five minutes away from the office. This was a clean, lovely house that he had just renovated and was trying to sell, and he and I would be able to live there among the new hardwoods and countertops until a buyer came along. I had gained a tranquil living space with, thankfully, a compatible soul.

Driving to work Monday morning, my mind rummaged through the list of things I had to do—work and later unpack my boxes. If I didn't do that now while I was in the mode, my papers and files would always remain a jumbled pile in the corner of the bedroom for me to feel guilty about. I also owed my father a phone call. He would love to experience this panoramic drive even just going from my house to the veterinary hospital. I could attempt to explain on the phone the mountain-rimmed skyline in all directions that swelled my spirits but I really couldn't describe it for the encounter that it was. In words, this was a generous meadow I drove around, but if he were here, he'd smell the air and his metabolism would kick up a notch and he'd be proud that I'd found such loveliness. Like the time I went out to Arizona to visit him and he took me to the Grand Canyon. There was no verbalizing the way the Natural Wonder sucker-punched me. My spirit was thoroughly saturated and my eyes drank in every pixel of color and space as I gaped. And when I later looked at the pictures in the tourist brochures, yes, that was what the Canyon looked like, but even the professionals couldn't capture it, the feeling. Those photos were beautiful, but only a fraction, one dimension, an inch of the mile-high experience. So I wanted him to feel this place, to absorb it for a few days. Dad had recently moved from the home where we grew up in Maryland to Arizona, where the air was dry and better for his lungs and he was happy as could be, everyone with their motorized golf carts, him playing as much of the sport as possible, but physical visits were few and far between. His weekly phone calls started with a weather report ("the monthly average high temperature in Sun City was seventy-five degrees for the month of March," as tabulated from the hi/low thermometer outside his kitchen window, which he compared to March in the White Mountains, "forty-eight average degrees cooler than in Arizona") and the assurance that he was having "just another day in paradise." My siblings and I were thrilled for him to find such happiness in retirement. Dad planned to fly out here this summer and I couldn't wait. Why, there was a client I'd become friendly with, Mrs. Flynn, who was kind and hospitable and lived outside of town. She knew the region's attributes. She'd just started coming to our hospital for her Yorkie's heart ailment. When she brought him in, she usually carried gifts of exquisite bakery bread or beautiful folk art she had crafted and once a bottle of wine. I could ask her for suggestions for places I could take my dad when he was here and surely she would steer us in the best direction. I still had a few months before his trip and dwelling on his future visit put me in a good mood for the start of my work week.

When I pulled in to the otherwise empty parking lot, I noticed Lois Nelson waiting in her car. Her door swung open as I stood from mine, a worried expression visiting her face. In her arms was a thick blanket, its contents invisible.

"I'm so glad you're here! I knew someone would be opening soon and this cat just appeared in our yard late last night. Look at the condition it's in!" She moved the blanket enough for me to see the bony forehead of a grey tiger cat, eyes open and blinking. "I don't even know if it's a boy or a girl. It hardly weighs anything! All skin and bones. Where could it have come from?" Lois was one of the earth's compassionate souls put here to help animals in a very special way. They seemed to find her, perhaps sensing a "free food" message written in pheromones by the last stray critter that found its way into her nurturing hands. I always told her there's a special place in heaven for people like her. Her care for animals was a top priority, even if this meant doing without in other ways to be sure financially she was providing all the animals needed. I had learned that her anxiety for the animals' needs was potent and her concerns often valid.

"Well, let's get him into the clinic so we can take a good look. Did you have the cat around any of your other cats?" I fished the clinic key out of my hand and juggled my overstuffed carryall, lunch bag and purse as we walked in.

"No. See, I didn't notice him at first but I figured out later that he must have been hanging around the back for a while because that afternoon, J.R. kept running to all the windows and the slider. He'll do that sometimes anyhow when he sees another cat or a rabbit. But then Titan, my collie, and Bandit, the other dog, were whining, sitting by the back slider and wouldn't budge. They seemed fascinated by something. I couldn't see anything outside. I finally went out and there was a cat, tucked just under the deck. Look at him!"

We were in an exam room now and Lois lowered her bundle onto the table. The loosened coverings unveiled the shape of a cat, tall and angular. His skin draped over his protruding bones such that he would have made a good study for an anatomy student learning how vertebra bones interdigitated in the cat. Yet, his belly was loose and saggy ahead of his rear legs, shaped like a cow udder. "Lois, this is a boy. It looks like he used to weigh a whole lot more at one time. I wonder if he got lost or ran away and hasn't had a meal in a long time. Or maybe he has an illness but no one has been treating him." How did this old man take care of himself wandering around on his own? He must have been fifteen years or older. His top canine teeth hung long and low, their tips dangling well below the lip line in a fine approximation of a saber toothed tiger. How did he find food? How did he find Lois? Thank goodness this weather wasn't as harsh as the previous months so he had a chance.

"Well, what's wrong with him? Is he going to die? I tried to feed him and he ate but then he threw up right away. I haven't been able to get him to hold anything down. I hope someone didn't just kick him out of their house because he's old and sick. Look how sweet he is!" He head-butted her hand with his forehead when she stopped patting him to talk. He certainly knew whom to endear to him, I thought. I could only imagine when she found him, bending over to scoop him up and croon softly to him. She probably closed him into her bedroom away from the other curious critters and put him on her bed to assess him for any sores. I bet she opened special cans of cat food and turned on soft music for him and put him on the softest blanket she owned. Lois's animals were as much a part of her world as the trees and grass, she'd once told me, yet they give back. They were never judgmental, she said, and they always expressed their affection no matter what she looked like that day, whether she wore her stinkiest gym clothes or her dressed-up work clothes for her bank manager job. Whether she'd driven a hard bargain at work or whether she'd won the lottery, the dogs were there, waiting for that walk. If she said something out of line to someone, J.R. still jumped up on her lap for some loving. And they all needed her, like this one, she emphasized.

I couldn't feel any tumors in his protruding abdomen to easily explain his emaciation. I told Lois that we should do some blood tests to rule out kidney disease, hyperthyroidism and diabetes, the most common elderly cat issues. X-rays would be necessary too to see if there was a mass in the belly or fluid. Maybe he even had worms.

"Of course, Monica, you know me. Do whatever he needs. Should he stay here for the day?" He was now a new member of Lois's clan. What a lucky boy. There would be no want for his next meal or fluffy pillow and tender spoiling.

"Yeah, I'll keep him, hook him up to fluids. It may even be a couple of days. Who knows how long it's been since he's had some good nutrition. Maybe we can get the vomiting to slow down with some medications to settle his stomach." I wouldn't have the blood results back for a few days, but I could at least boost him up and hope that was what he needed.

"You know, Lois, I hate to have this part of the discussion, but if he doesn't do well or his test results show me something serious that we can't fix . . ."

"I know, I know, but look at him! He still has life in him. He's rubbing. He purrs. He closes his eyes into little slits like he's happy when you touch him. He just doesn't move much. You don't think he's suffering, do you? I'll take him in and do whatever he needs, poor thing." She moved her thin frame next to his side and tilted her head close to his. "My heart's breaking to picture what he must have been doing before he ended up under my deck. Do you think he's been lost for a long time? How would I even go about looking for his owner anyhow?" We decided to see how his treatment went that day and take things a day at a time. We could revise our plan as we went along. She would talk to some neighbors to see if anyone knew anything about an elderly, tall, creaky-boned sweetheart of a cat missing from the place where he most belonged, an empty cat bed in front of someone's radiator. "You'll call me as soon as you know anything, right? You see how special he is, don't you?"

"I will Lois. You're good to do this and bring him in. If I were ever reincarnated as a cat or dog, I'd be coming to your house too, you know.

You're free to call and check in with Beth if you're worried." Which I knew she would because she would have this on her mind all day. "By the way, what should we call him?"

"I don't know, let's let him earn it. Tell me if you get any good ideas and we'll name him together, okay?" She waved as she left the building, just as Beth pulled up for the start of the day. Nick had told me he'd be later than usual that day, as he had a seven a.m. dentist appointment. I'd have to show him this cat's remarkable fangs when he arrived.

I saw Beth and Lois chatting in the parking lot, Beth's head side-turned and face sympathetic as she surely was hearing the sad story of our newest patient. I'd get started on his workup, and I knew by the time I was done, Beth would have come up with a list of imaginative names to choose from.

The cat let me do whatever I needed, lay on his side for his radiograph, offered little resistance while I drew blood, him a relaxed sandbag, happy to lift his chin for a scratchin'. "Are you sick or are you just sloth-like?" I put him on the floor to see how well he could move around. He extended his rump into the air, lowering his front half. One front paw reached forward in a lazy stretch, then the second. He lifted his chest, back arching now, to finalize the move with one back leg stretched out behind, then the second. He looked up at me and blinked, standing in one place. I heard his purr from where I stood. "Go ahead and move now, sweet boy. I know you can do it," I said in a soft voice. He sniffed the air, as if deciding whether it was worth the effort for him to ambulate a few steps. In his mind, I guessed, the mental wheels were balancing the merits of calculated inertia versus curious investigation. Finally the new surroundings won out, and he decided to move, his overlong toenails clicking with each slow stride. "You know, you could use a spark plug to get you going, big guy . . . hey, what about Sparky???"

The door to the treatment area swung open just then and Nick walked in. "Good morning, Dr. B. Why, I thought you were back here talking to someone. I could swear I heard your voice. It's just you here. You know, only I'm allowed to talk to myself around here. You're too young to already be doing that." He chuckled.

"Hey, Nick. How was the dentist? I'm not talking to myself. I'm talking to the cat." I realized that probably wasn't much saner.

"Whoa, won't you look at that thing. He needs his own dentist. What's up with him?"

I told him the situation and what the plan was. He couldn't fathom how this cat at his age in that condition could have survived for any period of time on his own. This would be a mystery we may never know the answer to unless Lois could locate his owner. I wondered how hard she would be looking, as I was certain she would feel he had been under cared-for and he was in Eden at her house. I surely agreed about that.

The radio in the other room played "Walk Like an Egyptian" and I told Nick that this nameless cat could take heed from that song and pick up his pace a bit. At which point Nick thought Ramses should be the new name. He was over my head historically, and when Nick started discussing the ancient Egyptian reign of pharaohs II, III and IV, I nodded and pretended to follow the conversation.

I called Lois later in the morning after we'd done a quick cleanup and seen some appointments. The cat's X-rays were unremarkable and I even performed a belly tap to be sure there was no fluid. It was dry. We would have to treat his symptoms until the lab called us with the blood results. Meantime, we hoped to rehydrate him, worm him and get him eating. I thought we should keep him overnight due to the fluid administration.

"But what about him being alone tonight after you turn off the fluids? Do you think he'll be scared? But then if I take him home too soon, will he get sicker?" Lois didn't want him having one more day of discomfort, I knew. I was certain she was planning which room in her house she would keep him until he could be integrated with the others and whether to give him the extra wide litter box or the one with the lower edge. Scented or unscented? Would he want the radio left on or complete silence?

"Lois, listen, how about this? Let me take him home to my house tonight. That way, I can get some more fluids into him until I go to bed and keep an eye on him. You know I'll keep him comfortable and I won't let my cats bug him." I was really fond of him. "But we need to name him! We've got a couple good ones to throw at you. Beth likes Chewie, Ricky, Sprocket and Saber Toothy, calling him Saber for short." I added Nick's and my suggestions and told her to let us know what she liked so I'd know what to call him. She chose Sparky because she liked the irony.

It was a straightforward day otherwise with enough to do that my feet were swollen and my legs tired. It would be good to go home and relax. It wasn't my turn to take calls tonight, so things should be peaceful. David had to be away for a couple nights, so I was alone in the house, which would be great for the cat. I could give some good attention to Sparky. There was a good being in that cat body of his. My cats might be a little off-track about it, but they'd get over it and besides, it would only be the one night. I could keep Sparky in my room with me. Which reminded me—I grabbed one of the litter boxes we used in the cages so he'd be all set and I could close their box on the other side of the bedroom door for Amos and Moosehead to use. That should make everyone happy. Besides, my cats were still getting used to the new house, so they were hopefully in an adaptive mood. Sparky had eaten some food during the day at the hospital and held it down, thanks to the meds.

In two trips to my car, I loaded up: Sparky in Lois's carrier in my right hand, my carryall bag on my shoulder and my purse. Then the bag with Sparky's medications, his fluid bag, litter box and a couple cans of cat food. I placed our patient on the passenger seat and told him what a handsome boy he was. It was so nice having the new car, which had a bit more room to fit items like the carrier so it wouldn't tip at an angle, comfortable seats and windows I could roll down from the driver's side with a touch of the button. I cracked the window on each side to circulate some of the cool air for Sparky. As I shifted into reverse, I tried to think what I had at home for dinner and realized it might be a good evening to stop by the village store for a sandwich, which Peg, one of the owners, served fresh from the store deli selection. I could also pick up sliced chicken breast for Sparky—it should be gentle on his stomach. I would give my own cats a treat too and maybe they'd be less likely to oppose our guest's visit.

I turned right out of the hospital driveway and passed the town common on the left. The heartbeat of Norwich seemed to center around the common. This was a small triangular patch of grass that served as a hub for places important to life in this small town. Its angles pointed to my new home, to the animal hospital and to Thompson Lake Road, respectively. At the base of Thompson Lake Road, a stone's throw from the common, was the Norwich Village Store, a general convenience store, an essential part of Norwich culture. The small, wooden-floored establishment was the perfect place to grab most last minute items that didn't warrant a trip into Plymouth. I visited the store nearly every day.

"Hi Pat!" I smiled as I walked in. Peg and her son Pat owned the place and they seemed to be there a million hours every week. Early in the morning into the evening and open Sundays until about five p.m. I asked how on earth they handled all those hours and had a life. Pat said at least he didn't need to head in at two in the morning like I sometimes did. And besides, when it was quiet, they could read a book or relax a bit and there was a back room that was comfortable. I'd become a regular, in for a fresh lunch when the peanut butter sandwich I'd packed just wouldn't cut it, swinging by to grab the always-needed extra cans of cat food, picking up a quart of milk and dish detergent, picking up a Sunday paper. Pat was good to me, as was his mother.

"Hey, Monica, haven't seen you in a day or two. Where you been?" Pat looked up from behind the counter. It had been busy at work and I couldn't step out, even that quarter mile distance. I kept missing the post office hours too, so my mail must be backing up, I told him. The village store shared a storefront and a walkthrough to the Norwich post office. Since most residents rented a post office box and collected their mail daily, the shared complex was the place to see who was there, hear the latest weather updates and slow down the pace for a few moments. The first time I tried to find the post office, I attempted Beth's directions, those being that the post office was in the building next door to the convenience store. I repeatedly drove slowly past the village store, realized I had gone too far and turned around again. Back and forth I went, feeling like a cast member of the Twilight Zone since there was no other building next door to the village store. I remained unaware of the subtle signage in tiny letters proclaiming the existence of the diminutive mail center within the left half of the building. I finally found the post office when I walked in to the store to ask for directions, which Pat still liked to remind me about, telling me I looked like a deer caught in the headlights. "Yeah, are you sure you haven't just gotten lost on the way over these last few days instead?" He winked. "Got something for you if you want it. Clearing out the magazine racks and I know you like to read. Here's a ladies' home magazine and also *Fly Rod and Reel.*

"Thanks, Pat. Sure, I'll take 'em." That was nice of him. Maybe not what I would have bought or even thought I'd ever read, especially since I lacked in the domestication department and I was not a fly fisher myself. But I'd take them because he wanted to do something nice for me. I bet I'd even get a chance to flip though them tonight while I sat quietly with Sparky when I reconnected his fluids. "Hi, Peg, how are you? Tonight I wanted to pick up a sandwich for my dinner . . . any of that egg salad you make that's so good? Also, I'll take a half pound of the sliced chicken breast for a little sick kitty in my car I'm taking home." I described Sparky to them in case they knew of anyone who owned him. Not that I wanted him to be with someone other than Lois, but maybe there was a frantic owner somewhere from whom he'd wandered away.

"Have a good night, Monica. You look tired. Get some rest tonight." Peg sometimes gave a little mothering nudge to me. Just a little, ever since the time around the holidays that I'd rushed in, trying to leave town on time for a family reunion with my father and three siblings who I missed dearly. Not wanting to arrive empty-handed, and not having time to do anything else about it and still make my flight out of Manchester, I thought I'd see what was here. My hope was to find something that spoke of New Hampshire so Judy, Phil and Kathi could sense the beauty here. Not finding anything like that, and realizing that a trinket from the airport would have to do, my eye caught the "collector" sweatshirts just in time. These dark blue lightweights were emblazoned with "New Hampshire's State Bird" under the image of a mosquito. They would do. As I bought those three, I had explained to Pat and Peg about my incredible family and how bonded we were and how we always argued when we were kids but now we're really, really close. I just wished we saw each other more but we all lived so far away, which is what my mom and dad had done when they'd followed their careers and gotten married—moved to where their lives led them. It was at that point that I had unexpectedly broken into tears, greatly embarrassed, but I couldn't help it. The store was empty and Pat got quiet. Peg came around the counter and put her arm on my shoulder and asked me why I was so sad. I had apologized and told her I must be stressed and missed my family. She asked me again what was wrong. I had told her that my mother had died when I was five years old. Breast cancer. Every couple of years it hit me really hard and I just couldn't bear it if something were ever to happen to my father. That scared me. It seemed so unfair that I never had her to help us grow up and tell me all the mother stuff, like I was good enough and pretty enough. That she wasn't there to guide us and model for us the sharp wit she supposedly had. Everyone told me I was a lot like her in a lot of ways, but I wanted to see it myself. And my brother Phil, he was only three then and had no memory of her whatsoever. At least I had some pictures in my mind. Kathi and Judy remembered some. My dad was a wonderful man and had done a great job raising us and we had a nurturing live-in housekeeper, I told her, but you still need your mother, even when you're twenty-six years old. She held my hands together in hers and told me everything would be okay and that my mother would be very pleased with who I had grown into. She said that life has some terrible tragedies and some very rich blessings. It sounded like we had a strong family and there was nothing more important than that. I wiped my eyes and thanked her. Pat had at some point disappeared into the back to give Peg and I our privacy. I was so grateful to Peg, and that was the only time we had such a talk. It was pretty much normal business after that. But she was my unlikely counselor that one time, unassuming Peg, a woman of few words, who chose just the right ones that time and patched a little Band-Aid on my deep wound. Every time I stopped by thereafter, I knew she was looking out for me.

"Okay, Peg. I'll try to get some sleep tonight. I'm giving this poor old guy some extra care and looking forward to it." I felt good. I was tired but the feeling of a job well done brought satisfaction. Sparky seemed improved and I knew he would be spoiled from now on in Lois's hands if he got to stay with her.

It was good the days were lighter now, I thought as I drove home. Just a month ago, driving home at this hour was dismal. Now, I felt uplifted. Still cool enough out but better, much better. I put my finger into the front of the cage door so Sparky could sniff it. "What a good boy you are and we'll be home in about three minutes," I said in my singsong. "I think you're doing much better. You ate some today and we'll have some more at my house. A little more fluids in a couple of hours and we'll be all set." How fortunate that he was a peaceful car-rider, I thought while I drove. Some cats in cars turned almost demonic. I took my hand away and seconds later, Sparky made a retching sound and let fly a projectile heap of vomit. It smelled of the cat food he'd had that afternoon and most of it was in a linear streak on my new car's passenger seat and floor. I decided to pull the car over rather than try to make it home. It had seemed like such a good idea to bring him home, but now I bet the ride upset his stomach. Sparky would be all right, but I knew that bile could permanently stain upholstery the longer it sat. Ugh. I pulled over on a wide part of the shoulder in front of a large yard. What to do? I didn't have any paper towels with me. I walked around and opened the car door, telling Sparky what a good boy he was, poor thing. In my carryall bag there was a medical journal I wasn't done reading, but I probably wouldn't finish it anyway so it would have to do. I ripped the back pages from the magazine first, the classifieds for veterinarians looking for employees. I was all too happy to not be going through that search process again. The glossy surface on the pages made their vomit picking-up capability slippery, but at least it was something other than my hands. I moved the sandwich and chicken and used that brown bag Peg had given me to dispose of the mess. There would be more to clean up with a cloth and water when we got home, but at least the bile wouldn't saturate as much.

I stretched my back after bending over and took a good look at the yard next to where my car sat. Large rectangular patches of soil carried no grass and were arranged in long, organized rows. This dirt looked tended and cared for. Why, this must be Tip Jacobs's yard. Nick had told me about him. Annually, this dear wisp of a man in his twilight years shaped his large front yard plot into a floral exhibition of exquisite magnitude and proportion. This must be his template, land that he was preparing even months ahead. Nick told me that during the summer, Tip tended his gardens each day, starting at four in the morning and spending about four hours before the heat of the sun came. Just wait, Nick had said, and I'd see a gardening phenomenon of every color, every flower. The blooms would change as the weeks went with their seasonal nature. But always organized and always beautiful. What a treat to Norwich residents and travelers through town, Nick said. I couldn't wait. He said I'd never see a display like this ever again in my life, the result of one man's generous love of flowers. How good to be here. I bet this was something Keith's mother would like to see. I would be able to drive by here every day each way and notice. This brought new meaning to "stop and smell the roses." In my trying to not smell the vomit, I had stopped and noticed where the roses soon would be in a couple months.

My evening was not peaceful. By the time I had cleaned up and de-stinked my car, it was getting late. Sparky was to be king for the rest of the day and Moosie and Amos were wary. They skulked around, walking low to the ground, sniffing the air, following me around, humble servants plotting against their master. Sparky stayed in my room, quietly resting, where I had set up the litter boxes as planned. He looked comfortable on my blanket and listened to my radio while I fed the other cats and ate my own super supper. I loved Peg's egg salad. Barely any mayonnaise. Yuck to mayonnaise as far as I was concerned. It grossed me out. It was past time for me to give Sparky another bolus of intravenous fluids. On paper, it had seemed like bringing Sparky home was the easiest way rather than me going back to the hospital and sitting there for an hour while he dripped, but the way it was turning out was not what I had anticipated.

I closed myself in my room upstairs to hook Sparky up again. There were problems with his catheter. Whenever he pulled his front leg back, the catheter kinked, stopping the fluid delivery. I had barely read the letters to the editor in one of the magazines Pat had given me when I realized I would just have to hold Sparky's leg out in the extended position until his dose was done. He purred and purred. I flipped through the pictures in the magazines. Meantime, the natives were restless outside the door. Moosie, who constantly sought my lap when I was home, must have felt displaced. He mewed on the other side of the door as mournfully as the loons on the lake. I was glad David wasn't here. He hardly knew me and now he'd think I was being mean to my cats.

"Moosie, I'm in here," I called in what I hoped to be a cheerful, soothing voice. "You have to stay there until I'm done with Sparky's fluids." It's not as if he understood my words, yet I still spoke as if he could. My voice soothed him but he started up again when I stopped talking.

Then Amos joined in the fraying of my nerves by pulling at the door from the outside in an attempt to overcome his lack of opposable thumbs. When I looked at the door, a fuzzy grey paw reached underneath from the outside and swept along, sometimes grabbing the door toward him and rattling it. Two upside paws made an appearance and I imagined him rolled on his back. I called to him but he was persistent. I opened the door, at which point Amos turned his head as if I startled him, nonchalantly licked his paw and walked away. In a couple of minutes, he returned to the closed door and switched tactics to one of his tried and true techniques, usually used on me in the middle of the night from this side of the room when he wanted me to wake up. He stood lengthwise and stretched his long body, reaching for the doorknob with his paws. In his futile attempts to turn the knob, hope springing eternal, he leapt at the handle repeatedly, his paws sliding slowly down the length of the door. I tried to ignore him and read about the finer points of choosing the proper patio furniture. Amos continued his hijinks from his standing posture, no longer directed solely at the doorknob and he reached and reached repeatedly at the door panel like a hamster on an exercise wheel, willing the door to open. Early in his developmental months, when I was an exhausted veterinary student, Amos had learned that this technique was a surefire way to wake me up, whether it was for attention or to get to the other side of the door. But by his doing this, I had to take action, even if that involved my extreme annoyance. A water pistol by the side of the bed helped some but not much. One of my classmates in school had confessed to me that he too had a similarly mischievous cat who woke him one time too many and one night ended up marching the cat into the shower stall and soaking him to teach him a lesson. I'm not sure if his problem was solved or if I'd do the same but sleep deprivation creates desperate solutions. Because I was away at the vet school so much as a student when he was a kitten, sometimes even overnight, he had developed attention-seeking issues. I never thought about that at the time I took him in, as I had been moved with pity at his need for a home when he was an abandoned tiny heap of fluff with a ruptured cornea at the vet school and I thought surely I could balance it all. I also never thought at the time about the impact on my housemates in the places I lived. I'm sure his middle-of-the-night act was no fun for them either. It was also in the wee hours when I'd let him out of my room that he destroyed with his claws some of my housemate Jane's nice dresses hanging in her closet.

Thankfully Sparky remained unbothered by the ruckus on the other side. Indeed a mellow cat by nature it seemed or perhaps a tired old man.

I stroked his shoulder area. He was finished with his fluids for the night and I disconnected the drip bag where it was hooked on a knob on my dresser. It was two hours since we'd been home and I thought it time to bring out the deli chicken breast and get to bed. Amos and Moosehead were happy when I emerged and even happier for their treats. I wondered how this was going to work all night long but figured I'd spend some time playing with those two, fill their food dish again and hope for the best. For the most part, that was a good plan, though both of them ignored me when I tried to interest them in a wrinkled wad of paper or the beam of a flashlight. I held them each for a time and decided to call it a night. It seemed now they were satisfied and went off to wherever it is that they go during the day when I'm away.

We slept, Sparky at my feet in Moosie's spot, and Amos at one point tried the doorknob routine from the other side until I threw a pillow at the door from my side, too tired to come up with another idea. In the early morning, something woke me, and I looked at the clock, glad there was another hour to sleep. A foul smell reached my nose, and I sat up to see Sparky, sitting grandly on the floor, having filled the litter box with a large deposit. It was a proud moment for him. Could my nose ignore this and get back to sleep, I wondered as I tried to doze. The answer was no. Sparky was now a free man, and he decided to finish the job, covering and scratching like a good cat should. I was awake. There was no way around it. It would just have to be one of those coffee days but weren't they all. And I was on call tonight. Ugh. Maybe the heavens would bless me with a quiet one. I would get up, shower, clean up Sparky's business and maybe get in some of my own unpacking for a bit before heading in.

When I lifted the litter box, I saw that, even with his best attempts, some of Sparky's urine had landed outside of the litter box and soaked through the newspaper below it. David's new floors! Oh no. And my very first week here. What would he think? At least it was fresh, I calmed myself, using one of my towels to sop it up. I'm glad I didn't fall back asleep. I'd have to clean this the way I cleaned my car seat and rug. I was getting some good practice. Poor Sparky. It wasn't his fault. The other cats were glad when I packed up Sparky and opened my bedroom door to them again. Their noses were actively seeking the source of the great new scents. I prayed that Amos had used his litter box and not the wall through all this. He was one for urinating on the wall sometimes, or bookcase or important papers. His bad habit was so much better after I discovered a certain scoopable litter, unscented, no hoods on the box, always clean, always two boxes around, but even then, he sometimes expressed himself in that most unwelcome way. Indeed, he was my problem child.

Sparky arrived at the office with no gastric distress and he ate once he got there. His jaws worked slowly but functioned well. Work went smoothly that day. Lois was glad to hear that Sparky was improved and we decided she should take him back. She'd talked to a few neighbors and no one knew who he was. Perhaps this would always remain a mystery. I hoped so because now he was on easy street for the rest of his days.

His blood tests were unremarkable, no flags to explain why his body was so thin. His belly must have been full of worms because that quieted after his meds and as his good nutrition took hold. Perhaps he'd been on the road for a very long time. What a wonder that he made it to Lois.

The early edge of summer arrived suddenly, once Demeter finally decided to smile upon the region. Spectacular weather stayed with us, the pearl in the oyster. Clear air and low humidity were the norm and the joy of walking outdoors with no jacket on my arms was unbeatable. The wildflowers and greenery visible on the field enroute to work colored a pretty palette usually reserved for how-to painting shows on TV. But this was the real thing. Over the months, Lois and I talked many times, sometimes when she was in with one of the other animals and other times about Sparky. He was an excellent addition to the Nelson crew. He would never be pretty, she said, but what a sweetheart. And the other animals didn't bother with him. Lois apparently loved flowers and ever since I told her about the incident that helped me notice Tip's garden plot, she told me the names of the current blossoms emerging as I drove past, like the irises and peonies making their appearances. She told me to watch the choreography as it changed through the weeks and that she visited there often. It was already a spectacular sight and my dad would love to see this when he came to visit in a couple months.

One morning, Lois called, crying. Sparky had died in his sleep during the night. He had been fine the night before and had eaten well.

She'd woken, and he was lying on his side at the foot of her bed with no warmth left to his body. She had slept through it. I told her it must have been something sudden with his heart and that he surely never knew a moment's discomfort when he died. Tears welled in my eyes as I reminded her how his short presence had sparked us all. He was just really old, maybe even ancient, and at least these last months of his life had been luxurious. She would bury him there in the yard, she told me, and she'd plant a rosebush over the area.

"Lois, what a good soul, and how good for him to have had you."

"I know, it's just so sad," she said, her voice broken. "The most special thing he did was to survive enough to get here where he never had to work hard again. It's just that you fall in love with these guys."

Peg's words came back to me. Sometimes life gives you rich blessings.

# TEN

## *HARLAN*

Harlan was the third vomiter I had evaluated that day. The other two were likely to heal well on medication and bland diets. Their conditions were stable and their comfort levels fair.

Harlan, however, struck me differently. A normally proud German shepherd, his head now hung down, his energy drained. Standing up was too much of an effort for him and I winced as I watched him settle his chin onto his front legs where he rested. During his exam, he turned to look back at me when I felt his belly, a sign he was tender where I touched. Despite his discomfort, he still nuzzled my hand gently when I stroked his black head. I felt uneasy. One of the toughest decisions for me to make as a practitioner was whether a dog was vomiting because of a potential object wedged somewhere in the intestinal tract, requiring surgery to remove. Often these were painful, but so were some other nonsurgical conditions, like an inflamed pancreas, and it could be difficult to differentiate.

"Reverend Spencer, see how he's flinching when I touch this area? Could he have eaten something that he shouldn't have?" I sat back on my heels where I knelt next to Harlan, keeping one hand on his body.

"Why, I can't think of anything," he reflected.

I had met the reverend in the veterinary office only once. In our polite discourse, I hoped to implicitly convey to him my own admiration for his choice to lead an openly spiritual life by profession, surely setting a fine example to those in his community. My own religious upbringing was important to me and I tried to live and work a life reflecting this. I wanted to connect with that part, for instance, let him know how important were my "little prayers" each day—God, please help me find this vein; help me be a good doctor today; thank you, God, for this gorgeous scenery; help me have a better day tomorrow; bless my hands in surgery; bless all the anesthesias we do. I wanted Rev. Spencer to know that my spirituality was an integral part of my makeup. The fact was that I became increasingly more prayerful as the need arose and I felt pretty needy a lot of days.

"When he was a puppy," the reverend noted, "he liked to play with socks and towels on the floor. But he hasn't done that in a few years." One of his hands maintained constant contact with Harlan's body on the side opposite of where I touched. I imagined a calming force flowing through the preacher to his dog.

"Could he have raided the garbage? Do you feed him table food? Any high-fat meats given in the past few days, like steak or pork? Does he run through the neighborhood ever?" An accurate history was an important part of the investigative work.

"Hmmm, no." Dressed in his black suit and white collar, Reverend Spencer conveyed a tranquil, reserved aura. I imagined great, deep, inspiring thoughts to which his parish was privy during his weekly sermons. If he didn't such live a distance away, I could try to go one Sunday.

"I can't think of anything else, doctor, but I'll check with my wife. I've been a bit tied up with parish duties lately, so I haven't been home as much as usual." His soft-spoken tone clearly and precisely enunciated each word. I wondered if this was his nature or part of his training.

Harlan had resigned himself to my poking and prodding as his large frame lay quietly on the floor. His brown eyes hardly moved, yet his brows flicked in response to my motions around him.

I explained to the reverend the treatment plan—blood tests, X-rays, intravenous fluids, an overnight stay—and gave my assurances that I would call with any changes. "We'll do what's important to help him get well. We'll talk about things each step of the way and keep you posted with any changes to this estimate." I was learning from Nick how early communication about fees was key, however, I still really disliked that part.

"Thanks, Dr. Bors. I'll be waiting at home to hear from you." He cupped Harlan's chin in his hands and I watched the reverend make eye contact with his dog.

Soon I finished with the afternoon's appointments and was able to start Harlan's treatments. "Oh, my good boy, we'll get you feeling better," I promised him as I drew blood. I threaded a catheter into another vein in his front leg for intravenous fluids and gave an injection of an antibiotic. Harlan simply lay there, leg extended as I shaved it, cleaned it, poked it. His tail tip paddled every time I praised him. I guessed that even when he was well, he was probably just as cooperative.

Harlan's easy temperament led me to muse while I worked about how much of personality was inherent—human or animal. Of course, the personality with which one is born can be either augmented or harmed by one's upbringing. I pondered the age-old nature versus nurture question as my mind compared animals I saw to human beings I know. What would Harlan be like if he were a human? Maybe he would be the suave, laid-back, funny type, like John, my best friend through college, with whom I could share most any of my thoughts. What would my sweet friend Karen be like if she were one of my patients? Would she, while constantly wagging her tail, lower her head shyly when she came into the exam room, cooperating fully and endearing us all to her, rolling on her side for a belly rub? Conversely, would the fearless, turbo-charged Jack Russell terrier turned human be a bungee-jumping thrill-seeker whose schoolteachers scolded to sit still? In my patients, I could see the entire personality spectrum. The laid-back type B—the lovely, plodding, older golden retriever who followed all her owner's instructions and reaffirmed the notion of why I went into this field in the first place. The more uptight type A—like high-voltage, tortoise-shell cats, known for their inability to ever forgive a perceived past veterinary office transgression even years before. The outgoing, the shy, the clever, the lovable-but-not-too-bright, and the plain old ornery ones. I was curious about those excitable types—pulling away, biting or jumping around—who exhibited an over-exaggerated response to almost any procedure, painful or not. Were they really feeling things more than the calmer ones? Was their pain sensation more or their anxiety higher? And why did it get that way? Was it the same way with humans when they were hospitalized? And how much a part did human anxiety play in their whole medical picture?

I looked at my patient fondly. "Harlan, you are a fine boy." I folded a soft blanket into his cage. His tail thumped a few times and he daintily licked the back of my hand. I kissed his forehead, glad he was just who he was.

Nick was in the kennel room tidying up the place for the evening. I spoke so he could hear me. "Well here's just another example of your theory, Nick, or to quote you directly, 'It's not the day job, it's the night job that gets you around here'." I peeked my head around the corner toward him. "I'm running some fluids tonight for a while and also need to take some films. My biggest concern is a pancreatitis or foreign body in this big guy. He's got a painful cranial abdomen and a low-grade fever."

"I'll help you take the X-rays, Monica. Let me just call Gail and tell her I'll be a bit longer." Nick hung the Dustbuster he was using back on its wall-rack and finished tidying the counter in front of him.

"Thanks, that'll make it go faster." I wished I had someone making me a full dinner. I hated cooking and wasn't very good at it either. I was sure they were having another of Gail's masterpieces tonight, perhaps pot roast and potatoes with carrots, homemade bread and her rhubarb pie for dessert. The first time I'd visited Norwich to interview with Nick, Gail had a turkey dinner awaiting me, complete with trimmings. While I was sure I would be welcome at their dinner table any time, it would have been awkward on a regular basis for Gail and Nick to feel obliged to invite me over, though there were occasions and celebrations we shared. Nick would likely emerge from the house tonight, though, with a dinner plate for me to eat while I was still working, courtesy of Gail, with a nice smiley face in her pen taped to the top of the aluminum foil cover.

I would be unable to give Harlan more than a preliminary dose of the fluids in the couple of hours he stayed that evening. It was not a good idea to leave him unaccompanied and dripping fluids in case he should chew out the tubing. Still, I knew that sometimes even a relatively small amount of lactated ringer's solution into the system could make a huge difference in an animal's attitude, so it was worth getting Harlan started tonight.

Before he went back into the house for his supper, Nick helped me review the films we'd taken.

"Well Nick, I think a pancreatitis is unlikely, that area looks good, no ground glass appearance. But what do you think of the stomach here?"

"I don't like that either. I'm not a hundred percent sure but you could be right about a foreign body." I loved the moments when Nick and I were able to bounce our cases off one another. I certainly needed his experience and wisdom much more than he needed my whippersnapper book-smarts but he led me to believe that I helped him immeasurably in his workups. Often, nuances, subtleties, false findings and real objects that remained indecipherable muddied the interpretation of an intestinal pattern on a radiograph. And using the equivocal results to decide whether an animal should undergo anesthesia and exploratory surgery was often an agonizing choice. I knew I'd have a restless night's sleep. Going through school, I never comprehended the burden of responsibility for such choices that I would feel once I reached the "real world" of practice. Thank goodness Nick was in town that week to lean on.

"Yeah, I think in the morning I'll snap another film and maybe pass some barium to see if it outlines anything unusual."

"Good thinking, doc. Now make sure you don't stay here too long and make sure you get your rest tonight." He hung his trademark short-sleeved, light blue scrub top onto a hook on the back of the kennel room door. Nick patted Spook, tucked safely into his cage for the night after a day on the prowl and sitting on clients' laps in the waiting room. Nick loved that cat. It had been a good day for Spook—the only trouble he had seemed to get himself into was stealing some cat food from the cage of one of our hospital patients who I had on the treatment table. Spook had jumped into her open cage and fed himself a snack until I noticed and shooed him out. Now he was tucked in tight, cozy in his cat bed on his baby blanket, eyes relaxed slits as he watched me administer Harlan's fluids.

Nick and I both hoped tonight's medications would solve Harlan's problem but I had the uncomfortable feeling it wouldn't be that easy.

In the morning, Harlan definitely looked perkier. After waking at three a.m., worried about him and unable to fall asleep after that, I was relieved to see him. He greeted me with an uplifted head and wagged his big tail when he saw me. He had not vomited during the night. I assumed the fluids had made a big difference and hoped it would last.

"All right, Harlan! You look like you're in better spirits today, big boy." I was still uneasy about the way the stomach area had looked last night but I hoped all was clear, especially since he seemed to be feeling so much better now.

Dashing my good hopes, the survey film looked the exact same as last night's. Now I knew we'd have to do the barium series today, and it was best to get it started early. Harlan calmly swallowed his chalky-tasting barium mixture without the usual fuss and head tossing that many of our patients display. Using a large 60cc horse syringe, we attempted to get most of the substance into Harlan, at the same time dousing our hands and drenching the fur around Harlan's mouth. He now looked as if dressed in a Santa beard while he swallowed his multiple syringefuls, leaving four towels coated in barium as we wiped. The barium would outline his intestinal tract, potentially highlighting foreign objects or tumors. This study also allowed us to clock the travel time from mouth to colon. Some of the more subtle partial obstructions or soft foreign bodies may simply slow the passage time without being visible with barium. Objects like cellophane wrap could just sit within the stomach, clinging to the stomach lining and causing trouble.

Harlan's barium X-ray series took a couple hours of repeat views to collect. There were set times in which to snap a film to judge the rate of clearance first from the stomach and then through the intestines. Fortunately, Nick was there with me that day, so my back didn't struggle alone to lift and place Harlan for his views. As we gowned and gloved for each with the lead-lined gear, I sashayed in the ball gown I told Nick I was modeling.

To my consternation, the study we made indeed revealed something odd in the stomach. While most of the dye moved down the intestinal tract at a normal clip, an unusual amount remained bunched into a creased shape in the bottom of the stomach. Ugh. Knowing what he would probably say, I showed Nick and asked him if he too thought it best that I recommend an exploratory. I hated this decision. Surgery was invasive and involved risks of anesthesia and opening the abdomen. But leaving something in there that wouldn't pass was worse and even life-threatening. Would Nick expect me do the surgery myself? What if surgery didn't find anything in there? Nick assured me that indications were, for the dog's sake, that the best route would likely be an exploratory. He reminded me that sometimes dogs have negative surgical findings with nothing abnormal found, and that we were making the best decisions we could with the information we had available, so to go with that. And he would be there to help me in any way I wanted him to.

Relieved, I next called Reverend Spencer at the parish office.

"Well, there is good news in that Harlan seems to be feeling a lot better on the medications. The bad news is that we're suspicious of an object stuck in his stomach—perhaps a cloth of some sort? Anyhow, Dr. Schatzle and I think an exploratory surgery would be important for him so we don't miss something if it's there. If something's in there, he'll just go right back to how he was feeling yesterday."

"You guys know best . . . do what he needs." Rev. Spencer seemed thoughtful as he consented to the surgery. This seemed to be the best choice. Now I hoped Nick and I weren't wrong about subjecting Harlan to the risks of anesthesia and surgery.

"We'll probably do the procedure just after lunch. I'll be doing the surgery and Dr. Schatzle will be monitoring the anesthetic. I'll call you when we're done. I'm pleased with how stable he seems; the fluids have helped. He should do fine. You can say a prayer for us that all goes well." I didn't tell him that I always prayed inside my head before surgery. Today with Nick by my side, my confidence was at its best. I felt like one of the racehorses I used to hot-walk at the Bowie Racetrack the summers of my college years—heart rate up, prancy and nervous but ready to perform.

With Harlan anesthetized, we placed him on his back on the surgery table, clipped the fur off his abdomen and scrubbed the area with sterile soap. I realized that I had, like Nick, developed an important sense of the rhythm for the inhaling and exhaling patterns of the anesthetized patient, like the driving beat of a song. If Harlan's breathing slowed down, a silent alarm would trigger within our consciousness. At that time, most general practices did not have equipment bearing all the bells and whistles and beeps of a veterinary college anesthesia department. Pulse oximeters and blood pressure monitors were not available or affordable for small practices, so we needed to rely on our own assessment of the patient. Because of the schedule, one of us would usually be seeing appointments at the time another was doing surgery or one of us would have our day off. Consequently, each of us performed surgery alone, trying to remain conscious of the breathing pattern of the animal. It was a treat to have Nick "minding the store" in that regard so I could fully concentrate on the surgery itself. Nick was used to autonomy for the ten years he was a solo practitioner before I arrived, but I knew he really enjoyed the times we could share the experience. Harlan's respiratory rate remained steady and stable and I remained my most relaxed possible, thanks to Nick's proximity, though that was simply a lesser shade of anxious.

I donned a surgical mask, scrubbed my sweaty hands and slipped on a sterile gown. Gloved up and psyched up, I laid out the surgical instruments on the covered tray table and draped off the parts of Harlan's body that would not be involved in the surgery. Nick kept a close eye on Harlan's anesthesia level.

I incised the skin in a long, midline incision. I could do this. I had progressed quite a bit since first starting out—finding the linea alba, the "white line" that veterinary surgeons are supposed to cut to open the body cavity, was much less frustrating than it used to be. Breathing in the papery scent of the surgical mask that had snugged itself to my nostrils, I opened the body cavity with the scalpel blade. Once inside the abdomen, I was happy to quickly locate Harlan's stomach. I felt its thickness, bringing it to the inner edge of the body opening with some effort. Nick's assurances did me well.

"Nick—I definitely feel a wad of some sort in here. I'll cut it out if you can catch it for me. Want to place bets on what it will be?" This was exciting now. We probably were on the right track indeed. It was like finding you'd picked the right answer on a difficult true-false question in school.

"I'm always wrong, but I'll say plastic wrap—you know, could've been covering some juicy leftover roast beef gravy in the trash can."

I guessed we'd find a disposable wipe of some kind.

I cut through the stomach lining, like cutting into soft rubber with a sharp knife, the stomach wall thickened from irritation. Wedged amongst the stomach folds was a black, unidentifiable article of cloth.

"Nick, could you pull this out for me, please? Can you tell what it is?"

Nick reached for a hemostat, as excited as a boy collecting earthworms after a rainstorm. "Got it—I'll rinse it in the sink . . . oh, Dr. B, guess what it is! A skimpy pair of lacy black women's panties. This is what I think you'd call a *string* bikini . . . not that I'd know or anything. I'm just guessing, you see." He wore his impish grin. "Boy, these are kinda . . . well, let's just say I never would have guessed these to be the culprit in the reverend's household.

"No way—let me see! Well, I'll be! You know, we have to be very professional about this when we talk to them. Maybe he has a teenage daughter or they could be the wife's . . . you never know who wears black lacy things!"

We both laughed while I sutured together the incision on Harlan's stomach. Now I felt light and airy. The surgery was a success and it all came together so well. Most importantly, Harlan should feel better. Nick had helped me stay in control of my apprehension.

"That reminds me of the time I removed a pair of pantyhose from a dog's stomach. One leg was going up the esophagus, one down the intestines, and the body of the pantyhose was in the stomach," he recounted. We exchanged stories of many of the interesting objects retrieved via this circuitous surgical route—the Labrador he met who had a couple dollars worth of coins in his stomach along with nuts, wings and bolts; the cat who ate a portion of a telephone cord; the prophylactic found in a dog's intestine during my surgery rotation in vet school; the cat who swallowed a piece from a child's game so that when I incised that portion of the intestine, a yellow plastic smiley face beamed up at me.

"Well, why don't you call and tell the reverend what we found?" I was hoping to get off easy here.

"I'm not gonna call him—it's your case, Dr. B . . . but I do want to eavesdrop on how tactfully you do it," he snickered, clearly enjoying this. "I should get out a tape recorder!"

I shook my head, grinning and wincing at the same time. Why, I'd just glide right over it and that would be that. Diplomacy was usually in my court.

I finished suturing up the stomach, then we flushed the area with sterile saline. Nick's wisecracks made the time go quickly and I reminded him that we were to make no judgments.

I sewed shut Harlan's body wall and skin and felt suddenly exhausted. The worry over making the right call about whether surgery was necessary and the worry over the technical performance of the procedure drained me. At the same time I felt good. We had been able to help this dog in an illness that would not have gone away on its own.

When I called the house, the preacher's wife answered the phone. It was the first I'd spoken with her.

"Hi, is this Mrs. Spencer?" I asked cheerfully.

"Yes," she answered flatly.

"It's Dr. Bors at the animal hospital. I just wanted to let you know we've finished Harlan's surgery. He's doing fine and starting to wake up."

"Oh, that's good." Her voice was crisp, businesslike.

I paused. I wanted to sound upbeat.

"We did find the cause of his vomiting. He had a pair of black underwear stuck in his stomach. We removed it and he should do quite well." I hurried on. "Surgery went well. Anesthesia was good with no problems. We always watch afterward for signs of infection with any stomach or intestinal surgery. I'll probably keep him here another day or two, depending on his progress. Do you have any questions?"

She was silent. I wasn't sure if she was still on the line.

"Mrs. Spencer?"

"I'm here."

"Well, a family member can call in the morning and check up on him. Of course, I'll call if anything comes up sooner. Any questions?"

"What size were they?"

"Excuse me?"

"What size was the pair of underwear?"

Uh-oh. I felt my diplomacy medal losing its gleam. My having mentioned the color of the undies was definitely not a good thing.

I quickly countered, "The tag would be worn through from the digestive juices, so I can't tell you that. If you want me to, I can save them for you," hoping to sound easy-breezy casual, like no big deal.

"No, that won't be necessary." Her voice was brisk. I wondered what she looked like, the expression on her face. Was she paled, was she clutching the phone cord or running her hand through her hair?

Changing the focus back to Harlan, I told her, "Harlan's a really great dog. We all love working with him. Most dogs aren't as cooperative as he's been. I'm sure his great attitude's going to help him heal well."

Silence.

"Well, I'll give you an update in the morning, Mrs. Spencer. Good-bye."

Relieved to be off the phone, I told Nick about my conversation. He chuckled at the can of worms that Harlan may have opened.

That evening, as I administered Harlan's injections, he raised his sleepy dark head and thumped his groggy tail against the cage floor. I smoothed the fine hairs on the bridge of his long nose.

Could it be that in one retrieved foreign body and one terse response by the person I supposed did the family's laundry and who surely knew all their wardrobe contents, I was unwittingly privy to an unspoken family drama? One in which perhaps some little ministry bubbles were bursting in my mind? Or instead could it be that I had a wild imagination and that, besides, it was none of our business, Nick and me. Things weren't always what they seemed. Regardless, we are all vulnerable, all human, even those who are highly spiritual beings.

I had earlier projected onto the reverend an image of what I wanted my own faith to stand for: strength in times of worry (hadn't that borne itself out with Nick's help?); clear-headedness in times of indecision (hadn't the aid of the barium series helped us to know?); and peace within (hadn't I enjoyed this surgery far more than any other tough surgery and couldn't I find that place within me in the future?). None of those blessings had changed. All of it rang true. It was thankfulness I felt now.

"Harlan, buddy, you rascal, you. Whose secrets are you protecting? You've got me thinking too much now!"

He thumped his tail faster and nuzzled his handsome, innocent head into my hands.

# ELEVEN

## *BENTLEY*

Keith and I did not often share the same weekends off and most weekends, weather permitting, whoever wasn't working traveled to the other one's magnificent side of the state, I to the coast and he to the mountains. In my many visits to Keith and therefore his veterinary hospital on the seacoast, I became part of the staff's extended "family." I tried to lend a hand and make myself useful while waiting for Keith to finish up his Saturday morning appointments. Theirs was a large staff of mostly women with whom I shared a common sense of humor and affection. Lindy had been employed there for many years. She had seen it all and had been responsible for breaking in several novice veterinarians who started out there. I too learned a lot from her whenever I was around. She was more than adept at the required technical skills and Lindy willingly assisted new veterinarians and technicians in acquiring these talents. Procedures like placing an intravenous catheter or drawing blood from a fractious cat were made easier under Lindy's direction.

She was a sounding board to the unconfident: "What would the other doctors do in this case?" or "Can you think of anything I'm forgetting?" Lindy was clever and experienced and she generously offered all the glory to the veterinarian in charge, even when it was she who had gently reminded the doctor to look under the cat's tongue for the anchored thread causing its vomiting. If there ever was a misunderstanding in the client's eyes or phone call not returned quickly enough, Lindy rectified the situation by reflecting that upon herself. She termed it the "smart doctor/stupid technician" syndrome. I respected her highly and hoped Keith recognized on a daily basis what a treasure he had in her.

Keith's and my weekends were much better when we had each other around. He wore a pager on his waistband when he was on call, unlike in Norwich where there was no pager capability or even push-button telephone technology and Nick preferred it that way anyhow. On the seacoast, as long as we stayed within a fifteen-minute radius or so, the pager allowed us the freedom to go out for a bite to eat, hang out with Keith's parents and all their animals or take his parents' three dogs for walks on my most favorite Rye Beach. Keith's parents lived just miles away in picturesque Stratham and we shared meals at their character-laden, creaky-floored farmhouse, originally built in 1725, with a huge yard featuring Alice and Malcolm's peaceful English gardens. I became part of the clan as readily as one of the eight adopted cats living under that roof, each cat with just the right sob story and each cat with its own food dish in its own partition of the long cubby-holed wooden feeder Malcolm had built to make mealtime easier. The cats lined up like workers at office desks. Fat Badger, for instance, had been willed to Keith by an elderly client when she died, a twenty-five pound wonder of modern medicine who was the fastest mouser of the bunch, and Moosehead had just appeared there one day, a Tom Cat Special, unneutered and battle-scarred, wary of sudden movements, but he sweetly attached himself to me as a lap-warmer and companion when I was around. That is how I came to be his final owner—we bonded. And besides, the two of us shared the link of Keith's family's welcoming us into their fold. Eventually I took Moosehead to Norwich with me, where he would prove himself a loud purr maestro once he relaxed into the new haven he had found.

Keith and his brother Ian rented the window-encircled upper floor of a small beach house across the street from a strip of Hampton Beach where Keith and one of his coworkers tended lobster traps before work each summer. There was something quite sexy about Keith, in his orange fisherman's slicker suspenders over his well-muscled bare upper body, pushing his boat to shore. My one excursion on the boat to help pull traps in the ocean tarnished *my* skin tone green and proved me pathetically unappealing as I repeatedly vomited over the side of the boat, then begged to be brought back to shore, vowing to never leave land again. Just like the memory of the orange marshmallow Circus Peanuts that rendered the same effect on me as a child, I will never have an appetite myself for lobster fishing again.

My cat Amos started living in the house there on the beach with the brothers instead of with me in Norwich when he inappropriately urinated on several of my housemate David's blueprints for his contracting jobs in the newly renovated house where we lived. Amos must have realized he was on probation, as he behaved himself better there than ever before, with only one wayward urine pool found in a pair of Ian's old smelly sneakers, but Ian was gracious enough to tell me he was about to throw them out anyhow.

It was there in the beach house that Keith cleared his throat and silently handed me a box in which an engagement ring rested. I still made him say the words and I skillfully answered yes. After almost four years together, he believed.

Keith's and my time together went by too quickly. An otherworldly fog regularly met my seven a.m. Monday arrival in Norwich after a weekend dragged to its last possible moment with Keith, me leaving the seacoast well before any signs of life or the sun even hinted its waking. Wispy, dewy freshness wrapped its arms around my car and swallowed me whole. I was back. A by-product of the region's geographical location, Norwich in a valley among the mountain chains, this cool mist occurred in fall or spring, its delicious smell clean and innocent, eventually burned off by the rising sun. The nearly transparent atmosphere blessed my passage into its realm, sprinkling my windshield with its holy water. I sucked in my breath from the misty chill as I slid out of my car into the stillness of the hospital parking lot but then my body stepped up its metabolic rate and I warmed. It was Norwich's greeting kiss, welcoming me back to its fold.

One Monday, winding down the day's appointments, I received a phone call from Lindy.

"Hey, Lindy! How's it going? To what do I owe the pleasure of this call?" Just hearing her voice allowed me a connectedness to Keith.

"Hi, Monica. I have a big favor to ask. My ex has a really sick dog. He lives up north, about forty-five minutes from you, where I used to live. My former boss there has been treating the dog, but there are no easy answers. Anyhow, I just feel like you'd do a more thorough job working the case up. The other doctor is a great guy, but doesn't get quite as enthusiastic as you or Keith might. If anyone up there can help, it would be you."

"Lindy, you flatter me. I appreciate the vote of confidence and I'd be happy to help out. Who knows, I may be consulting with you and Keith there anyhow. What's going on with the dog?" I was honored, but wasn't sure what I'd be dealing with. Sounded exciting.

"Well, his name is Bentley, a basset hound, about seven years old. I guess he's having periods of being unable to get up and acting lethargic. It's the oddest thing. Gary and his wife Diane were pretty much set against a referral to Tufts or Angell," she told me in a clinical tone, as if presenting me a case study.

"Are there any test results?"

"Yea. I'll make sure Gary brings the paperwork down. Sounds like they were all normal."

"Hmmm . . . sending me a challenge. Have him call first thing in the morning, Lindy." As I focused on the pale blue wall by the phone, I imagined a sheet of paper as if in a textbook, a differential diagnosis for Bentley's set of signs, the potential rule-outs. I'd be making such a list on his record when he came in tomorrow.

"Thanks! And hey, Monica, I saved you some of those fabulous Lindt chocolates from the client of ours that works at the Lindt factory. She brought a whole big bag again and I know how you love those. Hid 'em in a secret place for you, with some extra dark chocolates."

"Lindy, you're the best . . . thanks so much." The thought of those yummy round chocolates that melted in one's mouth with the smoothest of tastes made my empty stomach growl. Lindy always saved me some that no one else knew about. I wondered if there were any sweets in the cabinet at home. Certainly not that kind.

Bentley arrived at the animal hospital the next day. While the dog was alert and responsive, he did not move much. Gary assured me Bentley's personality was usually much more lively than this. I examined him thoroughly, pondering what "lively" referred to. He was a basset hound after all.

"He sure seems like a nice dog, Gary." I searched Bentley's mouth for clues, listened to his heart, scoped his ears, felt his abdomen. He lay there quietly, occasionally peering at me, otherwise gazing away.

Gary looked back at me over his shoulder where he leaned over Bentley. "He must really like you or not be feeling well. He's not very fond of the vet's office, let's say. I'm serious, I wouldn't let your guard down." I smiled. Gary's carpenter jeans were frayed at the bottom and hung loosely on his waist. A red plaid flannel shirt verified his occupation as a real live, honest-to-goodness north woods lumberjack like Lindy had mentioned. For the rest of that day, a certain Monty Python tune would reverberate through my head, enough for me to later teach Nick the lines I remembered.

I looked down at the photocopied records from his local vet that Gary had brought with him and tried to decipher the handwritten notes from the other doctor. Since Keith's tiny print was even tougher to read than this, I was practiced in the art. "His blood tests from the other clinic do look normal. His physical exam is completely normal too, as of this moment. I think it would be wise for me to repeat some blood work, test his urine, and do X-rays too. Has he had a heartworm test yet this spring?" I had been hoping that something on the blood results would have caught my eye, a pattern somewhere to give some direction.

"Yea, that was negative, I was told. We give him his heartworm pills every day, especially with all the mosquitoes in our yard. We're really in a woodsy area and he just loves to hang out in the front yard. You just go ahead and do whatever you think he needs. My wife and I really love Bentley and want to do everything we can for him." In the few moments since we'd met, I already liked Gary and his concern for his dog. I was excited to see how we could help.

"Well, nothing pops out right away, but let's see what shows up. Can you leave him with us here? It may even be a couple days, depending on how he's responding." I smiled, hoping to put him at ease.

"Sure—can I call later?"

"Of course. We'll keep you posted every day. And I'll be working with Dr. Schatzle too. He and I always confer on our hospitalized cases. We'll put our heads together."

"Lindy tells me he's in good hands and I know you'll do what you can." Gary knelt on the floor and hugged his companion.

My thoughts swirled with the possibilities. Diseases that might not show up on the routine blood tests to cause his signs. It was like a quiz in class. What about the periodic weakness brought on by Addison's disease or what if he's been spitting out his heartworm preventative and had a hidden case of heartworm disease? Or if he had heart disease? Muscular weakness, back pain, cancer? Pancreatitis or liver disease? Could he be hypothyroid even?

Bentley slowly followed me on his leash. With some coaxing and even more patience, we eventually made our way down the hall to the treatment area. I lifted him with a grunt onto the X-ray table where I'd first start an IV line and draw blood. Because of Gary's stern warning about Bentley's temperament, an extra-large muzzle for extra-floppy jowls was part of Bentley's jewelry for those few moments, though he didn't growl or lift his lip at me.

"Bentley, you're heavy. I don't need the gym today," I told him, "and look how much you're shedding." He cooperated perfectly while I chatted at him. I scratched that area on the front of the chest under the neck that seemed to signal a dog that we were friends and that I wasn't trying to dominate him. He possessed typically difficult basset veins, the kind that curved over and around their short, stubby legs. His were already bruised from his original doctor's treatments. I knew I had been lucky to have obtained my samples and placed a catheter first try. Future blood draws with those veins would probably become more and more challenging.

A foot away from Bentley, I readied some X-ray cassettes, starting with views of Bentley's chest and abdomen. His symptoms were not classic of back pain, but it was something to look for, given his breed. Bentley seemed to enjoy my steady stream of language while I worked, asking him what he thought was wrong, informing him of our game plan, singing the lumberjack song to him like a lullaby, asking for his cooperation and how we could best get along, though he'd been the perfect patient so far. Indeed, he just lay where I placed him, following me with his eyes and his permanently furrowed brow.

Nick moseyed past as I completed Bentley's workup. He had just returned from lunch and was contentedly rubbing his belly for effect.

"Gail made the best chicken marsala last night and I enjoyed leftovers today for lunch. Hey, whatcha got there, Dr. B?"

"Hi, Nick. I took in this interesting case at lunchtime. He has periods of collapse and lethargy that go on for days." I was animated. "He doesn't eat well during these spells and he's still not quite right in between them. Otherwise, no cough or sneezing—doesn't appear to be painful. No vomiting or diarrhea. No excessive drinking or urination. With him collapsed, I wanted to rule out whether he's neurological but you may need to help me do a full neuro exam, he's so big." In my head ran images of Dr. deLahunta's Friday twelve-thirty p.m. neurology rounds that I attended faithfully, hoping to absorb even just drops of this instructor's brilliance, where he presented to an overflowing crowd of vet students the clinic's most interesting neurology cases of the week. Dr. D., in his commanding fashion, taught us again and again how to localize the neurologic lesion through a proper exam, which included "hopping" a dog on each of its legs individually, a difficult task on a large dog, so I would have Nick help me lift. I thought of Dr. D, wishing to do right by him, hoping to meet his high expectations for his students. While a student could feel small compared to Dr D's great discipline and his encyclopedic command of all things neurological and anatomical, clearly he was a man of deep compassion. The last week of junior year, my father was suddenly hospitalized from a heart attack the night before Dr. D's notorious oral final exam. Dr. D dropped everything, offered me a couple of exam options that best helped me through and allowed me to get home to Maryland to tend to my dad for the summer.

I continued my report to Nick about Bentley. "His heart sounds good. I got a good abdominal palpation, which felt normal to me. I can't find anything wrong on these X-rays . . . they're still wet, but maybe you could see if I'm missing anything. On his prior blood work, his electrolytes, chemistries and CBC were normal, but I'm probably gonna send out some other tests." I stopped, one corner of my mouth pulled down with a little frown as I pondered the clues. Sherlock Holmes? Not exactly. But I certainly hoped not Inspector Clouseau.

"Whoa! Now catch your breath. How'd you do all that already, Monica? Did you have extra caffeine, Speedy? Was I lingering over my proverbial sardines too long?"

I giggled.

"No . . . I was just excited to get this started. It's sort of a referral from one of Keith's technicians. These people live about forty-five minutes north of here. Seem nice. He wasn't hard."

"This sounds right up your alley!" Nick patted Bentley, who lifted his head when Nick spoke.

"I don't know. I'm feeling quite humble right now. I'm gonna have to put my thinking cap on. Do you mind please examining the dog too when you get a chance?"

"Yup-yup, sure." Nick nodded assuredly. I was glad for his help and loved our cooperative work together. Many times, the case belonged to us as a team and Nick and I had each other to hash it out with.

Bentley waited until after that first day to bare his teeth. I allowed him to be grumpy and slipped on a muzzle when using needles, just to be safe. Some days he seemed to respond well to the sweet-talk as I tended to him, enjoying our time together. Other days he simply hung his head on his front paws and ignored me. His demeanor in general was quiet. There was no question that he preferred me caring for him over Nick, as he lifted his lip in a warning twitch when Nick worked on him but with me, he usually relaxed. I figured it was because he had seen Gary and me together when he first came and knew that his owner approved. Nick said that some dogs liked a woman's tone of voice and that I was lucky in that regard being female but he also told me his singing voice couldn't carry the same notes, so I had the advantage. I told him he'd just have to memorize the words to more tunes.

Nick's impression was that Bentley sometimes held his neck stiffly, which made him think of a disk or spinal cord problem. The X-rays I had taken to outline that area were fine, but in general practice, we were quite limited in what we could see on plain films. We both knew that neck films were really hard to interpret and that, truly, at the time, the only way to outline what was happening with the spinal cord was with a myelogram, a specialized dye study, which had to be performed at a referral institute. I just couldn't appreciate Nick's finding or get Bentley to react to neck manipulation, although I paid heed. I had a lot to learn from Nick. Maybe the problem really was pain and not metabolic. With his breed's droopy temperament anyhow, perhaps the posture most other breeds typically exhibited with neck or back pain was masked in Bentley.

Bentley became more depressed and lethargic as the week progressed. He would barely eat, so we kept an intravenous line running. To run blood work from Norwich, we packaged the tubes and mailed to them to an outside veterinary lab, our only feasible way to get results as, to Nick's knowledge, we were not on any lab's courier route. He'd been doing it this way for years but it was often a couple of days before results were back. There were some very basic yet helpful tests we could do in-house and sometimes in an emergency, I'd even do most of the CBC by hand, using an old-fashioned special grid I'd place under the microscope, counting the number of white blood cells in a few of the boxes, then multiplying by a factor to acquire the total white blood count. All the repeat blood tests were completely normal and I had run some extra ones, certain that something would be flagged that I could zoom in on, but it was not to be.

I was stumped. Nick was stumped. We felt that we had probably ruled out a lot of the diseases on our list of differentials as best we could at our hospital. I called upon Keith's encyclopedic knowledge almost daily with over-the-phone updates and he was puzzled as well. I was so glad to have Keith to bounce my tough cases off, though it must have drained him when he was juggling his own caseload there. On most cases I asked him about, he found a unique twist, a new thought, a different reflection off the disco ball, one word that made the potential disease mechanisms click or one idea that confirmed my diagnostic suspicions. Here, however, the tangible was elusive. After four days, I had reached a point where I needed advanced help and would have to broach that topic again with the owners.

I picked up the phone handle, resting one hand on my chin and running my other hand through my straight hair. "Hi, Gary. Bentley's not much better today. I really think we should consider a referral to Tufts Vet School in central Massachusetts or Angell Memorial in Boston. Not that we're giving up on him here, but I just want to do what's best for Bentley." I pulled at a strand of my hair with my fingers. It was a really Bad Hair Day and no barrette contortion could salvage it. Maybe if I tugged enough, an answer would be pulled forth from my brain.

"Doctor, I really appreciate your concern. We won't go for a referral though. I know it would be more expensive then we could afford." He answered gently. I could imagine his down-turned eyes and mouth.

"I understand. They are expensive, but you get the opinion of the experts and tests we can't do here," I answered.

"It's not just the money. It's at least a three-hour trip each way for us. We know that you're doing all that you can. We want you to keep treating him there. You don't think he's suffering, do you?"

I thought for a moment. "It's hard to say in a case like this. When he's grumpy, I wonder if he's in pain."

"Well, you know, he gets that way even when he's well. Been that way since he was a pup, even with us sometimes. We call him the Big Bad Wolf when he's cranky." That made me feel a little better that his mood wasn't only the result of illness or pain. It was him.

"I sure wish he could talk and help us out here. We're still not even sure what body part is making him act this way." As I thought about it, I knew I probably wouldn't do anything differently if he were my own dog. How would I have been able to make the trip to one of the referral places or afford it on my tight budget? "Well, we may try some heavy steroid doses on him to see if that might help. We've avoided steroids so far because they can be a double-edged sword, helping pain and many immune conditions, yet possibly harming any infection or certain underlying diseases that might be there and we just don't know on him. However, Dr. Schatzle wonders whether there may be some back or neck pain, and if that's the case, he may get significantly better with their use."

"We trust your judgment, doctor. So does Lindy."

I instantly thought of her and her faith in me. I hoped I wasn't letting let her down. We'd surely keep trying. Mostly, I just wanted Bentley's condition to turn around. Gary and Diane had come to visit almost daily and were usually able to get Bentley to eat a bit of food they brought. Diane would take off the bandanna she wore, wishing to leave her scent with Bentley. Each time, Bentley nuzzled her and put his nose into her armpit. She and I agreed that it was good she didn't wear frilly dresses with all his slobber. Gary watched their greetings and then whispered secret things into Bentley's big earflaps. He left a flannel shirt for the dog to rest his head on later.

I enjoyed a friendly professional relationship with them and appreciated their honesty. I was, however, extremely frustrated by Bentley's lack of improvement and deeply disappointed in myself. Nick tried to tell me that there will always be some cases that we just can't figure out and that we just can't fix, no matter how hard we try. That's one of the hardest facts he'd had to accept over the course of his career. I had pored through all the texts on the shelf at the hospital and at my house, had pulled out my internal medicine notes from vet school to see if I could connect any more dots, find that one outstanding clue that we wouldn't be able to find without a more exhaustive set of tests. I felt like my tiny Datsun 710 I had through vet school, spinning its balding little wheels doing its best to make its way up one of Ithaca's steep snow-covered grades. What I needed was a roundtable of my teachers from the small animal clinic at Cornell, kind Dr. Randolph or intellectual Dr. Center or wise Dr. Moise or personable Dr. Tampke—as humbling as their verbal quizzing could be when I was a student on rounds, I could use a mini-version of each of them on my shoulders now, asking leading questions, imparting their special knowledge and whispering in my ear flaps what to do next.


It was my scheduled weekend off and Nick told me a trip to the seacoast would do me well. These past few days seemed like a month to me. All I could do was focus on this case. It was always in the back of my mind. Nick would be capable of caring for Bentley without being overly obsessive about him. I was too involved and felt too responsible.

Driving away, I shed the strain of this past tough week. In the rearview mirror, the maples and conifers lining the road seemed to gently wish me well as they waved in the breeze. I imagined those gorgeous mountain passes, the tip of Mount Washington still with a hat of snow on its head, now behind me, echoing their approval to the music of Lone Justice and Bruce Cockburn streaming from my car, with a little veterinarian's voice piping in. My brother Phil, a part-time disc jockey at a college radio station, periodically sent me new tapes of artists he liked. This music fed me, inspired me, amused me, helped me dream bigger and drive better.

I didn't visit Keith's practice that morning. Instead I slept in his bed while he worked, which was just as well. Later, I walked the beach, the ocean a powerful mood adjuster. In all its vastness and white noise there was room for only that which was there at the moment—the way my shoes felt as they sunk into the sand grains and the way my cheeks pinked as the stiff breeze nipped at them. The salt air pushed into my nostrils, like nature's aromatherapy, restoring harmony to my core.

When I returned to Norwich Monday morning, refreshed, Bentley was still there, but he was a different dog. Proud, standing straight in a run, interested in life, he was brighter than I'd ever seen him. His IV catheter was disconnected. His empty food dish bore witness to his newfound appetite. Nick hummed a tune as he hosed down the runs outside when I walked in. I trotted over to him.

"Good morning, Nick! What did you do while I was gone—a miracle? I can't believe Bentley is looking so good!"

"Well . . . I'm not sure you'd approve, Dr. B, but I went for the high steroid doses. He was a new dog in about twelve hours."

"You were so right, Nick! I could hug you! At least now we have the answer as to how to treat him even if we never figure out the 'why'! I'm so psyched!"

Nick's face beamed.

"We-e-ll, I'm just glad it worked out. How was your weekend?"

"Great—even better now. I feel like a weight's been lifted, Nick. You're such a good doctor! Have you told the owners yet?"

"Yeah, Gary was pretty happy. I told him it was your idea."

We walked back inside to the kennel room.

"Nick, you're too much. Well, what do you think of sending him home? He's been here almost a week now."

"Yeah, I think we can let him go today. You can see Gary or Diane out and explain the medications to them. They really know you most."

"Oh, sure. It'll be a pleasure. Thanks, Nick. I'm so glad you tried it." I wanted to break into a round of applause. Clearly this had been what the dog's body needed.

"Well, you know the saying about steroids, 'never let an animal die without the benefit of steroids',," he chuckled.

"I'm a believer for this case," I grinned. Next time I would be sure to listen to what Nick was trying to show me about developing clinical judgment, the kind where experience started to temper in. Sometimes as a practitioner, you had to take a step into the air, especially when nothing else was working.

I explained to Gary and Diane that morning that we didn't know exactly what we were treating, but it was likely a problem involving the immune system. Also, we still couldn't rule out a disk problem in the neck. We weren't out of the woods on this at all. Bentley would need to stay on the steroids for many weeks, if not his whole life, slowly tapering his dose to the lowest acceptable level for him. We would also place him on an acid-reducer to protect his stomach lining from the ulcer-causing effects of these steroid doses. They were to call with updates every two days for the first week until we felt we were under control.

When Bentley saw his owners, he whined while wagging his tail in a slow, constant pendulum. That was as excited as this basset got, Gary told me. It was good.

Diane's scarf stayed on her head today. We shared relaxed smiles as Bentley wound around Gary's legs in a slow ellipse. Trying to quiet the giddiness under the professional veterinarian lab coat, I could barely contain myself. I murmured my good-byes into Bentley's big flaps of ears. He nuzzled me, my friend now.

"I'm gonna miss the big guy. We've come to an understanding, him and me. Promise to call me if you need anything at all. Remember to call with those progress reports," I told them as I saw them out to the car.

"Monica, we want to thank you for everything you've done for Bentley. We're very pleased. Oh, and I almost forgot, we got you this box of chocolates. A little birdie told me how much you love 'em." Gary shook my hand as he handed me a box of the dark chocolate delicacies I loved. Nick and Beth would have to try these.

"Thanks, you guys! Well, we'll keep in touch. Bye, Bentley!" He was already settled into a comfortable spot in the back seat of the car. It was going to be a great day and week, I could tell. I was going to have to call Keith and Lindy and let them know the good news. I went back to seeing appointments with new energy.

In a little while, Gail stuck her head into my exam room. "Excuse me. There's someone on the phone that said he needs to speak to you right now. I don't think it should wait."

"Sure. Be right back," I told the owners with whom I was currently dealing.

Sometimes Gail helped out up front for an hour or two if Beth needed to run into town to make a bank deposit. Gail would balance some of the book work in the office room with the front desk responsibilities. There were no hold buttons on Norwich's rotary phones, so she left the front desk phone off the hook for me. I went to the back room extension instead.

"Hello?" I said.

"Monica? It's Gary." He was out of breath and spoke rapidly. "We just pulled into our driveway. Bentley jumped out, excited and happy, urinated in his favorite spot, and then fell over. He's dead!!" His voice broke.

"What!?! Oh no!" I exclaimed, shocked, shaken, not comprehending. "Are you sure? Can you feel a heartbeat on his side or see any breathing?!?"

"No——" He was sobbing. "He's dead. We're sure."

"Oh no! I don't know what to say." Cold ice flushed through my chest and I wanted to throw up. Gary tried to speak but couldn't.

I needed to get in control. I fixated on the phone cord, in complete disbelief. "Do you want me to do an autopsy on him, Gary?" I managed.

"No. We can't bear to take the drive back again. We'll bury him in the yard here."

"I'm just so sorry. I really don't understand. We thought we figured it out. Listen, call me later if you want to talk it over."

"Yeah . . . I just wanted you to know."

We hung up. This surely was a dream. My zombie-like attitude changed only when I walked out of the back room to realize that the front phone was still off the hook on the desk. The clients seated in the waiting room had been privy to the entire conversation, the high emotion and the end of the story only. Gail was doing paperwork in the office around the corner, having forgotten the phone and unaware of the situation. I walked up front and hung up the receiver. No one looked up.

I never recovered from Bentley's case and I learned to never take for granted when all finally seems right in the world of medicine. Of the entire laundry list of diseases we were capable of testing him for at that time, there was no conclusion. I was haunted by this case and became a more humble doctor that day.

# TWELVE

## *CASSIDY*

Cassidy was a great companion dog for my housemate David. Their similarities in high stamina and small stature sealed their bond. She was just six months old when I moved in with them and I delighted in this petite beagle's affections. She was silly but intelligent, energetic yet tender. Still, one had to prove oneself worthy to earn Cassidy's approval—being sometimes the person to fill her food dish, being reliably gentle in tone and manner, bringing treats that her finicky palate approved and being fondly accepted by her omnipotent master. Once her endorsement was granted, however, she was unconditionally loyal and loving. She maintained an independent edge, always alert and in tune with David's or my movements around the house. Often, out of the blue, a little wet nose would tickle me when I least expected it as her stealthy, curious frame snuck up to find out what I was doing. "Cassidy, you scared me!" I would exclaim and lift her into my arms, her mouth appearing to smile as she panted during the ensuing body rubdown she received.

David and I shared a tranquil existence, each of us moving in circles of understanding for the other's motivations. When our schedules found us home at the same time, he and I often gravitated to the kitchen table, philosophizing over a snack while the sleeping Cassidy lay curled at David's feet. Our friendship thrived on the insights and respect we offered one another. When I moved in, he let me choose which of the two empty bedrooms upstairs I wanted and I chose the one with the window seat the cats would love. He encouraged me to play my guitar and sometimes I sang him one of my songs. He laughed at my stories. David's only criticism ever was to ask me to use the cutting board and not the new marble countertops to cut my sandwich in half, and even then, he made it a joke. I liked that we could communicate. I loved hearing of his travels to Vermont, his plans to see Seattle. He described the trails he hiked with his girlfriend on the weekend, the spectacular tree they discovered in the woods with a rare type of moss growing on it and how Cassidy romped ahead and circled back, exploring.

David was one who thought globally and acted locally. I was one who worked locally and learned from him about further expanding my world concerns. I had been involved in hunger relief organizations in college and even traveled to Haiti, then thinking I might be able to use my future veterinary skills some day in a third world country but had lately lost that focus. David maintained that it was the youth that still carried a clear and active social conscience—our responsibility, even—and he aspired to serve in the Peace Corps. He reminded me how there was so much beauty out there and travels to enjoy, how he wanted to visit other countries and I found his free spirit inspiring. As a member of Greenpeace, he lobbied his congressman on environmental matters and made recycling a reality in our house, all cardboard and paper stored on the back porch. At age twenty-four, two years my junior, David had managed to acquire a broad range of worldly experiences with one idealistic foot still rooted in Norwich.

"You know," he said to me quizzically during a shared spaghetti meal, "there's so much to see and do in life. Why do people spend so much of it at work?"

"Are you referring to me?" I grinned widely. "It's hard to find a balance, isn't it? You know, my life's desire, my calling, has been to help animals medically. A lot of the old family photos have me holding the latest lost cat in the neighborhood. I devoured all the nature books we had as kids, and pored through the James Herriot series with a fire in me. I took every work opportunity possible to experience all aspects of the vet field. In high school and college, I put constant pressure on myself to keep my grades high enough for vet school. That desire never wavered. I couldn't see myself doing anything else. And now, I'm so glad I'm a vet but I get so tired and cranky sometimes. I guess it's all or nothing in a rural area like this, being on-call and working all these hours, and it's a lot of stress sometimes. Growing up, it was good to have that passion to make it, but I never thought about the stressful side of it or that there would be anything but joy each day on the job. Maybe this is just the way it is in real life in any job." I blew out a breath and watched Cassidy turn her head up at me. She came over and gently licked the back of my hand.

Sensing that his general query had stepped on a sore spot, David paused, probably realizing that this was a point for each to come to terms with in one's own way. The empathy on his face flattered his already pleasant looks. I moved down to the floor to put my arms around Cassidy, as she had placed her front legs on my lap, she an intuitve soother.

"Well, I guess I mean the desk job set—can you see me in a desk job?" We both laughed. Absolutely not. I'd never seen him dressed in anything other than jeans, shorts, and T-shirts, appropriate for his construction line of work. I could see him in the upper reaches of Arctic Canada saving baby harbor seals or in the North Sea boarding cargo ships full of toxic waste to prevent them from incinerating their loads in the water. I could see him in an African village, wiping porridge from an undernourished child's chin or helping run a grassroots vaccine clinic. But behind a desk all day? Never.

Cassidy's tiny sixteen-pound frame was hardly a distraction for David on his building jobs. She accompanied him daily, content to be a part of the team, resting under the shade created by the pickup truck's open tailgate, charming David's coworkers. She followed at her master's feet, sniffing out the new construction, granting her approval with a swing of her quick tail that all safety codes were met. After greeting each of the workers, satisfied that all was in order, she trotted back to the truck and found a cozy spot for her nap, David told me. Watching him hose off the truck after a day's job meant seeing her playfully chase the fountains he created for her with his thumb on the hose end.

Sometimes I came home from work to find David sprawled in front of his stereo speakers on the floor of his sparsely decorated living room, Cassidy stretched across his chest, soaking in some incredible music to which I was then indoctrinated. David loved music. There was barely any furniture, but there was a remarkable stereo system restoring, invigorating and exhilarating me too. It was there that I first heard guitarist Michael Hedges and I was instantly spellbound. David and I lay on our backs on his new hardwood floor, each in front of a different speaker, soaking in the fretboard mastery permeating our intellects. How could one human being conquer an instrument so profoundly and innovate to such a degree, we marveled? I played for David the mix tapes that my brother sent me, where we decided our favorites. I twirled Cassidy around, she being a willing dance partner to R.E.M.'s "Green" album. We discovered Kate Bush's thrilling vocal altitudes, heard the early Indigo Girl harmonies that I later learned every note of during my car rides to and from the seacoast.

David leaned his back against the wall, tossing a squeak toy for Cassidy and I slumped on the wicker chair while we debated such topics as whether our jobs define us or whether we decide our jobs' definition. Here was this young man, running his own business, relaxed, enjoying his evenings and weekends, in tune with causes bigger than him. Clearly, at the time, he seemed to have all his pieces put together. I sensed that he could be open to following another direction if it called him strongly enough. As for me, I told David, I felt labeled in the best of ways and happy for the tag of my profession. I had no plans to change that, of course, despite the job worries that I brought home with me, the self-critiques that played over and over in my head. Had I had made the right judgments on my cases? Concern about some of my tough cases wakened me at night. Perhaps it was a critically ill diabetic cat I had been working on that day or a dog that was recovering from a surgery I'd done—sometimes the drive back in to work in the morning seemed impossibly long since I could barely wait another minute to call the owner to check on the pet. David challenged me to get beyond those inner voices as time went on. He told me the same things that Nick had said, that I needed to believe that I was making the best decisions I possibly could but to accept that there were unknowns out of my control. I couldn't save every animal in my care nor could any doctor make perfect decisions all the time. And to know that I was a really good doctor.

Cassidy made her own contributions. She was not always effusive in her affection but she was always present, always utterly and loyally present. She frequently lay underfoot, arching one eyebrow as if to donate an opinion to the conversation in which David and I were immersed. Her head lifted sharply, her ears perked at attention while she stared in David's or my eyes, then she rested again on her stretched forelegs, her point well punctuated. Her fetish for my one pair of white strappy sandals taught me that I was not really destined to wear three-inch heels beyond the bridesmaid stint for which I obtained them. I assumed she was retaliating for my cat Amos's urine stains on her master's blueprints, ever loyal to David's best interests.

One weekend in the late summer, David wanted to go away to a weekend-long music festival at his girlfriend's college in Vermont and couldn't take Cassidy. I gladly offered to care for her. I'd be in town on-call that weekend. Oh, what fun I imagined she and I would have after my work hours. I was excited. I could take her for walks in the fields behind the house across the street. These were tracts of land I enjoyed exploring alone on my free days. A thin stream cut across the center. These several acres of sloping hills were enough for a good-sized walk around the perimeter. I absorbed the solitude of this isolated treasure whenever I could, identifying bird songs or noting the brilliant color flashes of the wildflowers. It would be great fun watching curious Cassidy explore one of my favorite getaways. David had her well trained to his voice and would often walk her off-leash in the woods and fields, but I knew I would take no chances while she was under my supervision and planned to keep her leashed.

Cassidy and I shared a cozy existence together our first day, especially her snuggling into my futon at night under the covers next to me, but we had little time for play. She seemed to accept patiently my comings and goings, even the two late-night calls. Each time I returned home, she lay resting in precisely the same spot on the kitchen floor she had been when

I left, waiting.

Cassidy needed a bath and her nails trimmed and I had told David I'd groom her in the office Sunday when the place was quiet. Even though rides in David's truck were royal carriage rides for her, Cassidy was loathe to step foot in mine ever since I took her in when I spayed her. However, I'd finally give her that really good bath I'd been promising David with one of the special shampoos we had at the hospital. In the raised tub there with the soothing warm water hose extension, she should be no trouble. She looked forlorn while wet but offered no resistance and I praised her profusely as I soaped and massaged and rinsed her. Her coat sparkled when I finished and her fur smelled like a delicious piña colada. After the bath I stuffed her collar and leash in my jacket pocket so I wouldn't forget them. I'd bring her home, let her dry some more and then enjoy a nice walk with her in those fields. Even if the ground was wet, we could stick to the higher ridges and she should remain fairly clean.

I bundled the damp Cassidy into a towel and carried her out of the clinic to my car. Reaching into my right-hand pocket for my car keys where I always kept them, all I could feel was the leash and collar. The door to the hospital was locked now, and I had the uneasy feeling that I'd left my keys inside, me here alone on a Sunday. I was pretty sure Nick was away this weekend too.

"Why did I even lock the car door?" I grumbled aloud. "There's no crime around here!"

Leaning against my car, I shifted Cassidy to my other arm to check my left pocket. She knew she was destined to go back into my vehicle, and I could feel her start to squirm. Unbalanced, unable to find the keys, my grip changed. With the ease of a greased pig and the speed of a scared rabbit, Cassidy capitalized on the moment and jumped out of my toweled arms. Staring after her in disbelief, my stomach in spasm, I watched her scamper across the empty hospital parking lot and down an embankment behind the lot, away from the road.

"Cassidy!" I called, "C'mon, girl!"

Oh, this was terrible, I fretted as I ran after her. Those must be all woods there. And lots of them. What if she runs off and won't come back to me? How could I have let this happen? Me, the captain of the safety patrols in sixth grade, nicknamed Miss Safety Monitor by my family growing up, who always wore my seatbelt, never swam within an hour of a meal, always looked both ways before crossing, always responsible, somehow unable to keep my housemate's little dog out of trouble for just two days. And she was wearing neither her collar nor tags. Somewhere through those woods was the bog, where there were beavers and the swamp and all sorts of wildlife, very cool indeed when a day hiker or tourist, not so cool when trying to locate a lost dog. I'd never be able to chase after or find her if she disappeared into the thick brush. She could be gone, gone. *Oh, God, please help me.*

I raced to the top of the embankment. At the bottom I could see the stream that I now realized ran all through Norwich's middle, the same one that cut across that peaceful tract of land near my house. Gee, I never even knew what lay beyond the parking lot, I thought. What an inopportune way to learn the local topography.

"Cassidy!"

I could see her by the stream's edge, sniffing the pebbles. At least she hadn't kept running. The filtered sunlight through the trees glistened on her back in a patchwork as it caught the shine from her newly clean fur. She sure was a pretty dog, even if she was being a brat right now. I picked my way down the steep, muddy slope, my sneakers providing just enough traction, small stones tumbling ahead of my feet.

"Here, girl, come." I said gently, now just a few yards away from her, a plastered smile on my lips. "Good girl." Every animal behaviorist I'd known emphasized the importance of making your "come" command sound sweet, pleasant and inviting. She knew what the word meant, for goodness sake. She was so well tuned to David.

Cassidy was having fun now. She lowered her shoulders and head, challenging me to a chase, and trounced her freshly washed legs through the cold water to the other side's muddy bank.

"Come. Please don't run away, Cassidy."

Argh. This was the worst thing possible. Losing an animal in any way, shape or form was the worst imaginable scenario for me. The notion of losing an animal to anesthesia when I was in charge, even when using the safest drugs possible in the safest doses, terrified me. Those cases were extremely rare, a few times in a vet's career at most, but always possible. Loss to escape was awful. I'd only ever heard about it happening to other people and now here it was me. And I had disregarded every precaution, let my guard and my careful ways down because I knew her so well. With a client's dog, I always, always used a double leash, slipping one of our blue nylon leashes on top of the dog's own collar and held both leashes looped around my wrist since sometimes the owner's collar was too loose. With Cassidy, I didn't even have her leash on. Never would I have thought she'd take off on me, not my little girlfriend dog. This was terrible.

I crossed the stream. There were not enough big stones above the waterline to let me cross with dry feet, so I too took the chilly plunge.

"C'mon now, Cassidy," I said, still softly encouraging her to come to me and reminding myself to stay calm, trying to keep a smile for her to see.

I knelt down to her level and put my fingers out, hoping she would think there was food in my hand.

"Oh, please, don't let her run off," I whispered.

Cassidy began to trot in the opposite direction. Now an antelope in the field, then a poodle in the circus ring, her lithe body demonstrated her athletic prowess, all the while moving farther away from me. With David, she would have stayed by his side. With me today, her mischievous spirit coaxed her to aspire to vast distances between us. In desperation, I decided to do what I'd seen David do when she was naughty at home, behaviorists be damned.

"Cassidy—get over here!" I scolded her, my tone suddenly stern, deep and firm, one she'd never heard from me before. I tried to sound as much like a momma dog's growl as possible, low and serious.

She stopped and sulked back to me, ears held down and tail between her legs. The game was over. I scooped her up and clipped on her collar and leash. "Oh, what a good dog! That's my girl, Cassidy," I gushed, my tone lilting and effusive, elated as the shepherd holding his lost sheep, the widow her lost coin. I carried Cassidy back across the stream, my feet squishing through the sloppy, freezing goo in my shoes. I picked my way back up the hill and to the car, holding her in an inescapable grip, talking softly to her. Head resting on my forearm, she resigned herself. She was panting and had her fun and I imagined a smile at the corner of her impish lips. I found the keys when I put my hand in my pocket this time. They had indeed been in the bottom there all along, tucked below the collar and leash. This discovery led to round two of sweet relief, for I wasn't sure at all how I'd have gotten into the clinic or my house were I locked out. I started to think through the logistics of what that would have meant were I truly locked out: Walking to the convenience store with Cassidy to call the police to help me break in? Walking home with Cassidy hoping I could find an unlocked window to climb in? Trying to find a locksmith on a Sunday afternoon? And I was the one on call that weekend. I realized how grateful, how very humbled I felt. Fortunately, the adrenaline panic during the chase had caused momentary amnesia regarding the potential lockout, so my stomach acid had only burned through one layer of gastric epithelium. Sweet-talking Cassidy the rest of the car-ride home, I accepted her muddy feet and belly on my jacket and the seat of my new car as her last laugh at me. A good toweling at home would have to do.

Enjoying the happy ending to our close call, I found the rest of that day pleasant. I walked the fields with Cassidy on her leash and let her explore the wetter areas—what the heck. She couldn't get any dirtier than she already was. Surrounded by nature, I tried to sidestep the uncomfortable "what-if-I-never-found-her" demons in my head that persisted. How many times would I scare myself thinking of all the places Cassidy could have disappeared to with no human attached? I pledged to give those voices no real estate in my mind this time. Cassidy was back and all was well. Nothing bad had happened to her. In fact, she probably had enjoyed herself. I was learning that I needed to keep busy when these thoughts came calling. And relax a little more. Yes, occupy my mind instead with good things, images I loved. When home from our walk, Cassidy and I would be dance partners to the snazziest album David owned. Then she would lay curled in the fold of my lap on the living room floor, tired from chasing the squeaky toy I'd tossed for her.

David returned from his weekend away with tales of late-night campfires and bongo drums, guitar players everywhere, songs free-floating. It was one of the best weekends he'd ever experienced. Surely, he said, I would have loved it and I'd just have to find a way to go sometime. I was glad his spirits were in a good place. He learned of our escapade and had to wipe the tears from the edges of his lashes when he finished laughing. From that point on, I was christened Cassidy's honorary guardian and she, my honorary god-dog. We three continued our special friendship for the remainder of the time I lived there and I never again tried to take Cassidy anywhere in my car.

# THIRTEEN

## *DANNY*

"Is this the doctor?" The man's voice on the other end of the telephone line was deceptively calm.

"It is," I answered, putting down the Sunday newspaper I had finally started reading as the afternoon wound down.

"This is Paul Martin. My dachshund's not breathing too good right now. Could you come in and see him?"

There are times when it can be difficult over the phone to determine the true nature of the emergency and whether the owner's assessment is accurate. This man's slow and unflustered speech didn't mesh with the situation he described.

"What's he doing?" I asked, sitting up straight.

"Well, I'm not sure Danny's breathing much. He took some water into his lungs . . ."

Assuming an urgent situation, I interrupted the caller to tell him to head over to the animal hospital immediately. He could be there in a couple of minutes, he told me. Fortunately, because I now lived in David's house, I could probably be there as fast as Danny's owner could no matter where in town he lived.

The summer sun was strong and the air warm with a fresh breeze. A floral fragrance raced in through my open car windows. It was a luscious time of year in Norwich. The weather had been dry, I mused while I drove, and I could not imagine how a dachshund could take water into his lungs. There were no puddles now and few people in town owned swimming pools.

I pulled into the hospital parking lot just ahead of Danny's owner, my heart racing. His car had been the one keeping up with my rapid clip the entire way to the clinic, which is how we each came to know that we lived virtually across the street from one another.

I quickly unlocked the hospital door and Mr. Martin carried the motionless dachshund straight into the exam room. Rapidly assessing the dog's condition, I saw that Mr. Martin's fears were valid. Danny wasn't breathing. I couldn't hear a heartbeat with the stethoscope or feel a pulse with my fingertips.

"I have to take him!" I managed as I lifted Danny's limp body and ran back into the surgery room where the oxygen was stored.

Danny's body was still warm. Automatically replaying in my mind the rote-memorized "ABC's of Cardiac Arrest" that all veterinary students are taught—A: Airway, B: Breathing, C: Circulation—my hands trembled as I inserted an endotracheal tube into Danny's windpipe, which would enable oxygen to efficiently enter the starved lungs. Starting the oxygen flowing, I alternated between performing chest compressions and pushing oxygen into Danny's lungs by squeezing the machine's breathing bag.

Pausing momentarily to listen to his chest, I could not detect a heartbeat.

"C'mon, little guy, you've got to pull through," I begged aloud as I restarted my efforts, calculating epinephrine doses in my head. I had met Danny only for his healthy vaccine visit that year. He was memorable . . . a sweet, middle-aged brown dog who was a pleasure for me to examine. I felt a heavy pull in my gut as I faced the looming reality that I would probably be unable to save Danny's life.

I continued my frantic efforts to revive Danny, trying to do the jobs of three sets of hands. I wished so much that I could magically transport Nick from wherever he was to here. But this one I would carry on my own—my own drug doses, my own decisions, my own intestinal fortitude. I became aware of Mr. Martin's presence behind me.

Over my shoulder, I acknowledged him, "How long had he been like this?"

"Well," he drawled as I continued my work, "I pulled him out of a groundhog hole where there was lots of water. I called you soon as I seen him not able to get up."

Groundhog hole? Surely I had misunderstood but clarifications would have to wait.

I had to get some drugs into Danny to stimulate his heart and breathing centers, but I could not afford to stop life-support efforts to place a catheter in his curvy dachshund veins to do so. Without an open line to his bloodstream, I remembered a less-than-ideal alternative with the respiratory stimulant Dopram: to squirt his measured dose down the endotracheal tube that was already in place in his windpipe. That I did. Nothing happened.

I hurriedly reached for the very important drug, epinephrine, hoping to jump-start the heart. There was an excess of epinephrine circulating in my own veins, but that didn't help Danny, I told myself, if I didn't stay in control. Knowing this drug must enter the body intravenously, I picked instead the desperation route—injection directly into the heart itself.

"Mr. Martin, you can turn away for a moment," I firmly recommended, not wishing the owner to witness this as a last memory of his dog.

Estimating the location of the heart based on where I normally hear it with the stethoscope, I quickly inserted a long needle into the chest at that spot and withdrew on the syringe. Good—there was blood flow-back. I was in. I injected, praying to jump-start the heart and then resumed chest compressions.

"You can turn back now," I said more softly.

I slipped the stethoscope back over Danny's chest. This time, my ears heard a beautiful, faint sound at the other end. "Lub-dub. Lub-dub. Lub-dub."

Danny's heart. The combination of the physical efforts, the oxygen and the seemingly "miracle drugs" had convinced it to function again.

Would it keep beating?

Despite my excitement, I held my tongue, waiting to say anything to Mr. Martin until I knew if Danny had truly started to revive. I stopped chest compressions, but continued to use the breathing bag to force oxygen into his lungs. I listened again—the beats were louder.

"Danny's heart has started," I told him evenly, moving my eyes up just enough to watch Mr. Martin's face.

Not expecting this, Danny's owner gasped loudly and his deadpan expression turned to quizzical surprise. So grave had been Danny's condition that I am sure, like me, he didn't permit himself to hope for more. Mr. Martin had been so stoic, so quiet the entire time he watched and this was his first show of emotion.

Within seconds, Danny's little ribcage moved slightly as he began to breathe by himself.

"Oh, it seems as if our little friend has decided to try to live a bit longer." I tried to be professional and hold in my giddy, elated feelings. I knew it just as easily could have gone the other way and we could still lose him anyhow. In those few seconds, though, I had undergone a metamorphosis from a harried resuscitator trying to perform too many vital jobs all at one time to a calm rehabilitator, quietly ecstatic.

Mr. Martin had suffered the agony associated with a sudden, tragic loss and was now catapulted into a new mindset, tears rimming his eyes and a weak smile on his lips. My wide smile encouraged his further.

Danny's vital signs held steady. His breathing efforts were strong but gurgly.

"We're not nearly out of the woods yet," I warned and he nodded, understanding the critical condition of his dog.

I was able to disconnect the oxygen tube after a short time when Danny began to move his head. Soon, he responded to our voices and was fully conscious thereafter. I asked Mr. Martin to pat and soothe Danny and he tenderly obliged me. Danny's large eyes focused on his master. I wondered if Danny was exhausted or if his spirit had floated above and watched us working on him, like humans who describe some near-death experiences. Was he frightened? Cold? I placed a catheter into one of Danny's front legs and administered intravenous fluids and other medications to maintain a proper blood volume and flush through his deprived kidneys. As I padded him in a blanket, I shook my head. This was amazing to be on this end of the resuscitation.

I looked up at the clock for the first time. It had been no more than twenty minutes since Mr. Martin had called me at home. I thought about who I was now as opposed to an hour ago. Older.

Mr. Martin was grateful, not gushy. Baseball cap atop his head, the small man in his late thirties seemed the kind of person who preferred not to draw attention to himself. He buried his hands in his pants pockets when not patting Danny, as if they housed a place to escape the extremes we had just experienced.

As Danny rested his head in Mr. Martin's cupped hands, I asked, "Okay, now what's the story here? How did Danny end up nearly drowning in a groundhog hole?" I had to know this, wanted to hear.

"Well, you see, it's this way, doc," he started slowly, stretching each monosyllabic word. The base of Danny's ears flicked upward in response to his owner's voice. "I been having trouble with some groundhogs in my yard. Digging big holes. Ruining my garden. Well, this afternoon I had Danny in the backyard with me while I was doing some house repairs. I go to the front of the house, right, and when I come back around, Danny's got his back legs wigglin' and tail stickin' up in the air with the rest of him down in one of them groundhog holes. That damn groundhog came up when I wasn't looking and pulled Danny in!"

His brow knotted while he pursed his thinly lined lips, pausing and blowing out a thin stream of air. I noticed the beads of sweat on his brow for the first time. I tried to picture this scenario, listening intently.

"I went running over there, knowing that damn thing was probably gonna hold on to Danny and by the time I got there, the dog was deep inside that hole and I couldn't reach him. Pulled in just like that. Well, I got my shovel and banged the ground to scare him to let go of Danny. Didn't work. Then I knew what I had to do. Grabbed the hose to flush out the groundhog. He would have to let go of my dog then. I turned on the water. In a very short time it worked and I could see Danny's tail coming back up to the hole. I reached in and pulled him out by his tail. He was all wet and I couldn't tell how good he could breathe. That's when I called you. Damn groundhog."

Then he was silent. His efforts to explain this bizarre happening seemed to use up Paul Martin's entire ration of words for the week.

I was numb. I glanced over at Danny's face and neck again. For all the work I'd done on his front end today, I hadn't noticed any bite marks or even so much as a scratch or cut. He was mud-covered, but no fight wounds.

I didn't know what to say. The truth of the matter, I was fairly certain, was different from Mr. Martin's interpretation of events. I remembered learning that the breeding of dachshunds for their hotdog-like body formation was, in large part, to chase and eliminate rodents and pests from the premises of their owners, who often lived on farms. Part of the breed's uniqueness revolved around the dog's ability to enter small places and track down varmints. I didn't have the heart at that moment to tell Mr. Martin that, in all likelihood, Danny himself had jumped into that hole to investigate, perhaps hoping to initiate a confrontation, and he would have surely been the victor in a scuffle with a groundhog. He may well have been investigating an empty hole. He surely would have worked his way back out of the hole in due time. If not, though, digging with the shovel would have been a much safer method of extraction.

I tried to look sympathetic and nonjudgmental. I tried to say nothing I would later regret. Basically, I wimped out, knowing that I would need to think about the best way to correct Mr. Martin's misconceptions without blaming him outright for nearly drowning his beloved dog. It was obvious that he felt he had done what he needed to do to free his dog. It was equally obvious that there was a profound bond between the man and his dog. How could I address the facts without making him feel foolish and devastated, without heaping guilt on his head? It had all been overwhelming to me too. I bit my lip and decided to mull it over.

"Wow," I said weakly.

Mr. Martin, satisfied that Danny had pulled through his ordeal and was in my care, headed home. I started the dog on antibiotics in an attempt to lessen the effects of the inevitable pneumonia following the inhalation of water and dirt into the air passages. Forearmed, I hoped, but also certain that reality would hit again when the second shoe dropped. I carefully monitored his intravenous fluids as well, trying to strike a fine balance between a necessary amount and overloading weakened lungs. I stayed with Danny for several hours more that night until I was certain he was stable and breathing well on his own.

I went home, spent. As I walked in the front door, the *Boston Sunday Globe* was spread on the kitchen table, mocking me. I slapped together a peanut butter and jelly sandwich and headed upstairs for bed, hoping the phone would remain quiet for the rest of the night.

We loved the thumping of Danny's tail on the cage wall whenever he heard Beth or me call his name from the other room. It hadn't taken us long to learn the special spots to scratch to elicit blissful facial expressions. Over the course of the next thirty-six hours in the animal hospital, Danny's cough changed from an occasional sputter to a wet, constant hack. He developed a fever. We all hated to see him feeling so sad, especially since he had quickly endeared himself to us. Chest X-rays confirmed the presence of a rip-roaring case of pneumonia. Nick, having seen animals come through various stages of pneumonia, encouraged me to remain optimistic for Danny's recovery. However, even he had never in all his years seen a case brought about in quite this fashion. Nick told me to keep the faith, especially because we had Danny on some very good antibiotics and together we were doing whatever we could.

"Can you even imagine trying to practice medicine in the days before antibiotics, Dr. B? Can you even imagine it?" He and I agreed that, as difficult as the field of medicine could be now, it would have been a completely different ball of wax then, wrought with frustration, helplessness and drastic means. I told him about my father who had survived tuberculosis that he contracted on board a Coast Guard cutter in World War II prior to antibiotics. My dad, in his twenties, had to undergo a permanently disfiguring operation, a thoracoplasty, which removed ribs and hunched his back, but effectively collapsed half of his lung field forever. This was so the *Mycobacterium tuberculosis* bacteria responsible for the disease would have no air available to it, which it needed to multiply. After two years of rehabilitating in a VA hospital, my father survived and eventually met my mother years later on an airplane. The four of us offspring owed our existence to that radical surgery. Though tuberculosis is still not an easy disease to treat, Nick and I agreed what a different story would have occurred in these times.

The worst symptom for Danny was the painful cough associated with his form of pneumonia. His entire body entered into the motion. A moist gurgle turned into a repeated hack, his ribcage moving and his abdomen contracting. We were attached to this brave survivor and whenever he went through these fits, whoever was in the room went to him, speaking softly, hoping to ease him, which helped. He then sweetly turned his face upward, tired, accepting a deep rub behind the ears, during which he lay on his left side and rolled his belly skyward, waving his right front paw. Beth surmised that Danny was right-handed.

"Nicest dachshund I've had the pleasure of keeping in the hospital," Nick told me. He challenged the right-handed/left-handed theory in Danny, keeping track with a chart on our chalkboard of the direction of the post-cough rub and rolls, and so far Beth was correct. In fact, he always rolled in that same direction.

Being in such a secluded region, there were no high-powered institutions within a three-hour drive to which Danny's intensive care could be referred, nor was Mr. Martin financially able. We would do our best, Nick and I, with Beth's help. Powerful antibiotics and intravenous fluids were staples of his treatment regimen. Every couple of days, we checked blood tests or X-rays to track Danny's progress. A chest massage technique, called coupage—basically a gentle pounding with cupped hands—was performed several times daily to loosen secretions within the chest. Because extra stimulation tended to precipitate coughing spells, the lights were dimmed at all times in the kennel room where Danny stayed and he was shielded as much as possible from loud noises. We placed a towel in front of his cage door and he slept on a thick, cozy blanket.

Danny, like Nick, was an optimist. While at first he had little appetite, I watched for steady improvements in that department. He soon enjoyed meals again. Early on his fourth morning of hospitalization, Beth chimed, "I just went to see Danny and he asked me to feed him, so you can skip his breakfast today."

"Asked you to feed him?" I laughed, "I just fed him before you got here! What did he do, that rascally little guy?"

The room's lighting showed off Beth's wholesome face, even prettier when she smiled. No need for makeup on those natural features, I thought.

"Well, he acted like he was starving," she answered, "First he looked up at me with those eyes. Then he pushed his empty dish to the front of the cage with his nose."

"That wasn't exactly a dish left over from last night, you know!" I giggled. I knew that mournful expression of Danny's.

"Anyhow," she said, "The best part was after I fed him. I stood in front of him, coaxing him to eat, which he did. When he was done, he rubbed my neck with his long nose and put his front paws on my shoulders. He was giving me a hug and a kiss!"

He manipulated us and we let him. "Oh, Danny," Beth cooed at him, "Don't you worry, we'll get you all better." He ate methodically, starting at the edges of the dish and working toward the prize in the center. Every several mouthfuls, he lifted his eyes to check that his caretaker was still watching, wagged a few strokes with his tail and continued his meal.

And so it went with him the next several mornings. Although we were on to his double feeding trick now, we let him think he was getting away with something sneaky. Nick had told me many times that there was usually hope if an animal patient maintains his or her appetite throughout an illness. Danny had kept up his strength through his diet, and the other therapeutic efforts could better do their job.

Thankfully, Danny did recover from his pneumonia. Mr. Martin visited daily, always coming on his lunch break and after work.

"Hello, Mr. Martin," I overheard Beth greet him one day from the front desk on Danny's sixth day with us. I was in the office eating my sandwich.

Around the corner, I heard Mr. Martin ask, "I brought Danny a hotdog. Think it'll be okay to feed it to him?"

"Let me check with the doctor," she said, popping her head in the door. I was already grinning widely and nodding yes as she peered in. I watched her facial contortions as she stifled the urge to laugh at his food of choice. Maybe he was pulling our leg or maybe that really was a favorite of his little guy. Either way, Beth was not going to let that slide.

Suddenly, we all heard a loud "bang, bang, bang, bang," coming from the kennel room in the back. Beth and I hurried toward the sound, wondering what disaster lurked in the room. Did Spook knock something over or were there sneakers in the clothes dryer? Opening the door, we saw an ecstatic ten-pound dachshund, swinging his tail wildly against his metal cage, having heard his owner's voice from the front of the hospital. His rear end was being swept from side to side as it followed his tail's movements.

"Mr. Martin, come see!" I called. Up to this point, despite the gains in his appetite and the sweet nuzzlings he enjoyed, Danny's personality had remained as subdued and stoic as his owner's. We were thrilled to witness, on this day, a sudden and dramatic improvement. Like waking from a nap.

He had reached a point where each initial cough did not lead him into an unstoppable sequence. His recovery had been steady and this was the sign we were looking for.

"Would you like to take Danny home today?" I grinned.

"I sure would," he answered, bouncing a bit on his heels.

I had come to know this modest man through the week. I admired his perseverance and quiet presence with his dog, how he lifted Danny's spirits each time he came to visit. We discussed Danny's home care and medication needs.

"You have to keep him very quiet for the next month while he recovers," I finished, "Leash walks only to go to the bathroom and then back inside again." I made some notes on the record. "Any questions?"

"When will the cough go away?" he asked thoughtfully, hands in pockets.

"Hopefully in a couple of weeks. There may be some lifelong lung scarring. This could seriously affect his activity level. We'll know as we go along. For now, no marathon running. You know to call if you have any problems."

As they left, I heard a deep-voiced stream of sweet-talk directed at Danny through the window screen. Humored, I peeked out to see Danny's ferociously wiggling body jump happily into his owner's car. I felt guilty that this entire week, I had managed still to completely avoid broaching the subject of the events leading to Danny's near drowning.

Mr. Martin headed back in to the hospital to see me.

"Thank you for all you've done, doctor," he said, shaking my hand.

"You know, I've been thinking about it a lot, and I might have been wrong about something."

Thank goodness. He'd figured it out. I didn't have to find a way to say anything more about how Danny got into this mess.

"Well, I was wrong to have left those groundhog holes open in the first place like that. I thought you'd be happy to know that I've spent this week filling them in so that ol' groundhog can't cause more trouble. I think I scared him away for good anyhow when I got Danny out."

Hmmm. Not the magic words I'd hoped to hear but progress nonetheless. I could still deal with this later when its impact might be slightly less painful for this caring owner. Or would I ever need to tell him? At least he was right across the street from me and I could keep an eye on my little buddy on his turf now and again. Hopefully we'd all be avoiding that damn groundhog.

# FOURTEEN

## *BABY*

"YIPE-YIPE-OOWOOO!!! OOOWOOOO!!!"

The small yellow dog began screaming the instant I walked into the exam room.

She wasn't bleeding, no one was touching her and she stood bearing weight perfectly on all four limbs. She stood squarely on the exam table, facing the far wall, extending her neck, howling with all her might.

"What's wrong?" I asked the owner, loudly enough to be heard above the dog's cries.

"She always does this—that's how she earned her name!" Theresa, smiling, answered above the noise. "Never been sick a day in her life. She's just here for her shots."

"O-WOOOOO! YIP-YIPE!!"

Noticing the dog's name on her record, I could see that the moniker Baby suited her well. The mixed-breed dog had been placed on the table by Theresa and all thirty-five pounds of her made a racket one would imagine from a dog three times her size.

"Baby, I haven't even touched you yet!" I coaxed, relieved to know we were not dealing with an emergency. I too now had a big grin on my face.

"ARR-ARR-ARR-ARR!" Her howls strung one into the other.

"Oh, this will go on for the entire visit," her owner laughed.

"She could win a prize for her acting skills, now, couldn't she?" We chuckled together.

I'd never heard of such a thing. What on earth could have triggered such behavior in the first place? I figured I should make this short. It would be tough to have a prolonged conversation above Baby's outcry. Besides, I was self-conscious about what the other owners—and animals—in the waiting room thought may be going on in this exam room. Surely Beth at the front desk would explain to the other waiting patients the situation. As ever, my goal was a peaceful experience, soft touch, calm patients. Many animals were calmed by quiet song-like words, a slow touch. I often approached from behind while the dog looked at their owner and rubbed over the hip area so they got used to me, or I scratched in a non-threatening body location, like the boney patch on the chest between the front legs on dogs. Fortunately, Baby was here for a routine visit, not for me to decipher mysterious symptoms of illness. Maybe I could still win her over. Once she knew that I would be gentle, perhaps she would relax. Her body language didn't display any aggression, no hackles, no pinned ears, no subtle posturing to concern me. Why would she do this? It was the oddest thing. It seemed as though her howls were to wall me off. I just wished her to understand that I was on her side of the fence. Baby avoided my face, not at all interested in the dog treat I offered her from the small pack I kept hidden in a corner of the treatment drawer. She looked straight ahead or at the ceiling, an avertive technique I called the "ol' fisheye" look. Other patients pretending they are not on my exam table also give the look, but most of these are silent protesters. Her vocalizations never ceased and their tone mutated shrilly as I softly stroked on her back, her pitch rising an octave.

"AH-YIP, AH-YOO! YOO! YOO! ARR! ARR-ARR-ARR!"

"Oh, Baby, I'm not going to hurt you, lovie!"

"Don't think you can sweet-talk her, doctor!" Theresa spoke loudly, grinning. She was clearly a veteran witness to this behavior. "Nothing works. The only other time she does this is when we give her a bath. Never, ever barks in the yard or when someone comes to the door. It's strange. She's been like this the whole ten years we've had her. I guess she's a bit peculiar!"

I nodded to Theresa, a sympathetic grimace on my face.

I worked quickly, looking at all Baby's visible body parts, peering into her ear canals, all the while maintaining my hand's constant contact on her frame. Her physical exam was completely normal, although an assessment of her heart and lungs above the racket was difficult, to say the least. Baby had herself so distracted that she never flinched for the small needles for her vaccines and blood test. I appreciated the earnestness with which she expressed herself. Every fiber of Baby's being, every hair that stood erect on her neck and back was immersed in her drama.

"Isn't she going to get laryngitis?" I called, in awe of this amazing performance. "YIP-YIP-YIP-YIP-YIP!" Her small nose pointed itself toward the ceiling as Baby stretched her neck for effect. Her upper and lower lips formed a ring as she sang.

"Well, we're all done." Despite my ringing ears, I had enjoyed this bizarre office call a great deal. Eight minutes earlier, I was uninitiated. Now I had encountered a delightful oddity. I wondered if Theresa's family warned the neighbors when they bathed her. Seemingly, all was accepted in good humor.

I walked out of the exam room and, like a switch, the noise abated. I proceeded to the reception desk to bring up the record. All eyes in the waiting room watched every move I made. Nobody was smiling.

"What a dog—craziest idiosyncrasy, huh?" I said to Beth as I handed her the record, my forced laugh loud enough for all to hear.

Baby trotted by on her leash, now silent and innocent looking as she sat obediently by Theresa's feet, leaning in. I could feel the waiting people looking at this small dog, then at me, then the dog. I felt them thinking: Somehow that veterinarian brought out the worst in this sweet, silent pup.

Oh, it was no use. "Who's next?"

Beth handed me a record. I looked up at the three clients sitting in the waiting room, two of whom were pointing to each other.

"It was the dog, not me, really!" I protested, grinning. "You tell them, Baby," I said to the dog, whose owner's attentions were directed toward paying her bill rather than defending me. I bent down as if to pat her.

Baby edged closer to Theresa's leg, silently giving me the ol' fisheye. I didn't want her howls to start back up again. "Sam Jacques, it's your turn," I said. Sam, tail held down, and his owner trailed me to the exam room.

"I promise it won't be so bad!" I said cheerily.

It was then that I noticed the exam room window had been open the entire time, allowing the Indian summer air to waft through the screen into the clinic and Baby's piercing howls to broadcast out through the neighborhood.

I luxuriated in the weather that allowed us to keep the windows open most of the summer and then once again into this lovely snap. Soon, there would be the brisk rush of air when the door opened and the aroma of wood stoves through the neighborhood. It had been one of the most perfectly temperate summers I had ever known—just right by day, never too humid. Tip's gardens had delighted me every day as I drove past. He even sold gladiolas as a specialty through July and August. People from all around knew about it and came to his little garden shop or just walked around to look at what he'd cultivated. Sometimes I stopped by and took snapshots in my mind. I couldn't even keep a philodendron alive, nor did I know most of these flowers' names other than the ones that we learned from the poisonous plant garden at vet school but I soaked in Tip's array. At night, when I needed a beautiful image to replace a troublesome thought, here was the perfect mental photo album. When stressed, I pictured myself standing there, the cascading belles of a foxglove plant in front of me or the pretty ridged petals of Shasta daisies, supposedly one of my mother's favorites, in the background. I put money in Tip's little wooden contributions box and hoped others did too.

Happily that summer, my father had come for a five-day visit. Not only had my dad seen the flowers but he saw Thompson Lake, which he loved, and I drove him further up the main highway to view the magnificent rock faces of Franconia Notch where he could say nothing but "wow." Dad stayed at a pretty bed and breakfast down the road from the animal hospital, and he quickly made friends with the innkeepers. As it turned out, that client I'd become quite friendly with, Mrs. Flynn, not only had ideas for places for my father to visit but she offered to drive him around the day I had to work. They had a ball, each as polite as the other, she a perfect tour guide. At the end of the day, he gushed about all that he experienced and how very nice people can be sometimes. The two of them enjoyed a pen-pal friendship thereafter and she sent him a lovely oil painting she'd created which he proudly hung in his new living room in Arizona.

# FIFTEEN

## *LEAVING*

As I turned the key in the clinic door for probably my last time, I wondered how my cats would adjust to the modest former sea-captain's cottage we soon-to-be newlyweds would be renting. The tiny weathered house sat on the very beautiful banks of the Swampscott River, close to Keith's office and over one hundred miles from these New Hampshire hills that I cherished. The fine old Victorian of David's that I'd be leaving was home to Moosehead's midnight mouse snacks (even if I did snatch his first one from him, squealing, only for me to sorrowfully let him finish the job since I couldn't end its suffering). Surely Moosie would miss the high-ceilinged rooms in which he'd napped, auditioning the perfectly angled sunray. My other cat Amos, temporarily staying with Keith these days, would luxuriate in this new home's most comfortably cushioned nook as soon as possible, and, in his free time, he would likely find new objects on which to inappropriately urinate.

Many times had Keith and I labored over the pros and cons of life on each side of the state, in the end opting to move east. Keith was already buying into a partnership at the seacoast practice. He'd worked there for years during summers and vacations and, besides, we'd be only eight miles from his family home.

I reflected on my year in Norwich as I removed my books from among the other reference texts in Nick's office. The late afternoon light filtered long shadows onto the bookshelves that stretched up to the ceiling. This room had been where I'd desperately searched for the antidote to a beautiful black Labrador's antifreeze poisoning, where I'd crammed into my head before surgery the technique and suture types needed to reconstruct that Sharpei's misshapen eyelids, where I'd begged God to help me find the answer to the sick but profusely-loved Siamese's perplexing blood results. In this room, I'd blocked out the world for a precious twenty minutes while eating my peanut butter sandwich on whole wheat bread. From this desk phone, I'd returned owners' phone calls, chatting first about their pet's difficulties, then many times listening as they shed their own personal problems—how much I felt a part of their lives. And, yes, there lay that damn answering machine which I had instructed half the week to disturb my restful times with its emergencies.

Nick must have noticed my car in the driveway. He came into the hospital carrying an empty wooden box.

"Maybe you can use this to pack your books, Dr. B," he said. "It was in the garage. You know how I never throw anything away that I might need later." He gave his usual chuckle and motioned his tilted head toward the attached carriage barn where he neatly stored his beloved treasures, many acquired during his weekly excursions to the town dump. Sometimes he returned from the dump with more in the truck than the garbage he'd originally left home with. Nick could see the true value in these castoffs too special to waste. I never was sure what he planned to do with the single large carriage wheel nor the huge anvil adorning the walls but he knew their potential.

"Hi, Nick! I was gonna come over to the house for my final-final good-bye after I was done."

He shifted on his feet, then gently placed the crate down next to me, "Have you got all your things? Your books? Your mug? Your stethoscope?"

"Yeah, thanks."

"Do you see any of these old textbooks of mine that you might want? You can have them if you'd like. Look, this one's from nineteen sixty-seven. A classic."

"No, thanks, Nick, I'm all set." I laughed a little.

He still sported a smile but the normal cheery edge was noticeably missing from his voice. His fair cheeks lacked their usual soft blush.

"We're sure gonna miss you around here . . ."

"Oh, Nick, I'll miss you so much. How can I ever thank you for all you've done for me?" My eyes fell from his to the old brown tiles on the floor. I needed him to know how much he meant to me. I know I'd told him how good he was to me many times in many ways, but I needed to express to him his impact, his influence, and how he'd helped shaped me, mentor me. I had entered my Norwich year a babe-in-the-wood with a broken spirit. Thank God I found Nick after that terrible first job experience. There remained painful memories of my prior boss. It was because of Nick's kind and gentle teachings that I could heal my soul and now leave Norwich with confidence in my own worth. By his example, he taught me how to talk to clients while projecting empathy and love for their pets, and that was really how he felt. I saw him day after day maintain a steady work ethic and support all my efforts. We worked as a cooperative team. Inside I wore a new pride in the fulfillment of yearnings that had dwelled in my heart since childhood.

"Well, since you came on board here, I've been able to get a reprieve from solo practice for the first time in years and I'm quite grateful. Like I've always said, it's not the day job, it's the night job that kills me around here, you know." We both grinned.

"It's the night job . . . now where have I heard that before?" I teased. I would just have to remember Nick's most famous sayings, each perfectly contextualized to capture the frustration of yet another overwhelming moment in practice. Coming from him, they didn't sound like whining, they just made me laugh. "Fun's fun" cheered us when we had to struggle to even slip a muzzle on an unruly dog or when there was some disgusting diarrhea to clean up from one of our hospitalized patients. "It all takes time" calmed me, helping me feel that it was all right when a chest tap or a cat abscess or routine lab tests took much longer to perform than I'd imagined. And then there was the sweet "thank you for all your good help" that I heard at the end of each day I ever worked with Nick.

"Before I owned this practice, I never enjoyed working with another vet like I did with you." Where he stood, his freshly combed hair captured one of the sun's fading rays.

"I'm gonna hate to leave here and start somewhere else. It's like ripping out this part of me . . ."

He helped me steady the pile I was stacking. Our somber spirits hung between us.

"Keith is such a fine character with a really bright future. You would be crazy not to marry him. He's nuts about you, driving two hours away just to meet you for your lunch break and then back home again on his day off! And your whole life is ahead of you—I want you to promise to call me if either of you need anything at all. Anything."

I smiled. "I promise." I thought I'd be crying, but I was dry. Damn it. Couldn't I even let him see how important he was to me, how he brought out the best in me as a person and a professional? Not the tears he saw when I was so frustrated in surgery and he scrubbed in to help me find the Rottweiler's abnormally hidden testicle in its abdomen, one that never dropped into place at birth. Not the tears when I was sleep-deprived from a tough weekend on call and I snapped at Beth and felt so bad that I hurt her feelings and Nick smoothed everything over. Not when the unpredictable calico cat bit through the fleshy part of my hand and he told me that's why he preferred dogs, 'cause you could usually see it coming with them. I wanted tears now.

He carried the box of texts as we headed toward the gravel parking lot. I opened the trunk to my car and tossed in the few items I held.

"You can put those here, Nick." His box fit in nicely and I watched as he reached to keep the top books from sliding out onto the driveway. I needed to speak my heart. Instead, all I could think of was the white running shoes on his feet and how he always swore they were the most comfortable shoes he'd found for our long days of standing.

I pulled at my too-tight ponytail and was chilled by a sudden gust of wind. Zipping up Keith's hooded sweatshirt that I wore, I felt warmer. My words were quiet, "You know, Nick, you brought me back from a terrible place . . . if I hadn't found you, I might have just quit it all, I think . . . I was defeated. You made me know that all that trying was worth it. You helped me grow and taught me to believe in myself. As if you knew what was inside me, my potential. Like I was a good doctor."

"You are! And don't you ever forget that. It's dreadful that anyone could make you feel any other way. I would take my animals to you in a flash."

"Thanks, Nick . . ." I looked down, flushed, humbled by his faith in me. "I guess I should go now."

We hugged, then I climbed into my car and backed out of the parking space. Nick stood outside the door of the clinic waving. His cheeks were wet.

# About the Author

Monica Mansfield and her illustrator, Sue Wilson, have been great friends since first grade. They dreamed of collaborating on a book together when they were eleven years old while walking the suburban roads of Bowie, Maryland between their houses. Dr. Mansfield knew she wanted to be a veterinarian since she was five years old, always attracted to animals. She eagerly devoured the works of James Herriot as she grew, impacted by the heart and honesty of these books. She attended the scenic Virginia Polytechnic Institute her undergraduate college years. The happiest day of her life at the time came when she received her acceptance packet to veterinary school, where she then hugged the surprised postman. She attended Cornell's New York State College of Veterinary Medicine for her D.V.M. degree, graduating in 1987. She ended up in her first year of veterinary practice working in the magnificent White Mountains of New Hampshire in a small country practice with a kindly older veterinarian as her mentor. Dr. Mansfield kept notes and held many of these stories of her year in those hills dear to her heart, which she finally committed to paper years later during an extended pregnancy bedrest period.

Dr. Mansfield works as a small animal veterinarian in Massachusetts. This is Mansfield's first published memoir, though she has been writing in various capacities since she was a girl.

Bean Pole Books
A Division of Southern Belle Books
PO Box 242
Midway, Florida  32343


www.BeanPoleBooks.net